CROSSROADS

CROSSROADS

your journey within

by Dr David Kaye

M

Melbourne Books

Published by Melbourne Books
4A/178 Collins Street
Melbourne, Vic 3000
Australia
melbournebooks@hotmail.com

The National Library of Australia Cataloguing-in-Publication entry:

Kaye, David M.

Crossroads : Your journey within.

ISBN 1 877096 06 7.

1. Self-realization. I. Title.

171.3

To my Family

An eye for an eye makes the whole world blind.

Gandhi

My being is a lens through which, people who come in contact view themselves. Most don't like what they see. In some, their image instills hatred. Only a rare few smile.

Anonymous

True words always seem paradoxical but no other form of teaching can take its place.

Lao-Tse

If the way which, as I have shown, leads hither seems very difficult, it can nevertheless be found. It must indeed be difficult since it is so seldom discovered; for if salvation lay ready to hand and could be discovered without great labour, how could it be possible that it should be neglected almost by everybody? But all noble things are as difficult as they are rare.

Spinoza

Be ye lamps unto yourselves.
Be your own reliance.
Hold the truth within yourselves
As to the only lamp.

Buddha

the author

Dr. David Kaye has worked as a Counsellor and Psychotherapist for over fifteen years, helping people with a wide variety of psychological problems ranging from developmental disorders, anxiety, depression, anger, pathological addictions, post traumatic stress disorder, disorder of the self, relationship difficulties and general existential issues. As well as being the Director of The Melbourne Clinic, Dr. Kaye works as a psychotherapist in private practice in Melbourne.

acknowledgments

I am grateful to Dr. David H. Malan and Dr. Arnold Lazarus for their tenacious and inspirational contribution to the science of psychotherapy. I am also grateful to my family and friends for their encouragement, enthusiasm and faith.

I owe a great debt to my patients who gave permission to use their real life examples for the benefit of others.

contents

invitation

This book is about finding answers to some very personal questions that most of us feel the need to explore to live a meaningful and satisfying life. Some people explore religion, some, philosophy, some, meditation and some, well, they give up. I am here to tell you that it is never too late to take stock and build a life for yourself. A life that strives to achieve satisfaction in all domains; health, family, interpersonal relationships, education, profession, finances and the self. A life that expends minimum energy to achieve maximum intrinsic and extrinsic positive gains in all life domains.

Understanding how to go about expending sufficient amount of energy to achieve a balance in one's life is a serious matter. Afterall, every moment that you exist, you exist with your past, present and future. If the past contains burdensome experiences and learned inappropriate behaviours, you are likely to bring your past into the present wherever you go and whatever you do in your life. This book is a good starting point to understanding some of these challenges. It is about love, hate, confusion, failure, success, conflict, peace, animosity, friendship, sacrifice, freedom and the essence of the self. In fact, it is an expose' of some of the things our parents, family, school and society generally forgot to teach us. It is about things that somehow disappeared between the cracks.

To be realistic, it is impossible to cover all of the vast number of potential problems we might encounter during a lifetime in a single book. The problems covered have included some of the more troubling, intractable and complex difficulties experienced by most of us who attempt to achieve a sense of balance in this crazed and unbalanced world of ours.

I would be delighted to hear about your experiences in applying the ideas contained in this book to yourself. If you choose to share your experiences with me, you can write to me at the following address:

Dr. David Kaye
P.O. Box 316 Flinders Lane
Melbourne Victoria Australia 8009

introduction

If only we humans were always happy and contented, if we always learned quickly, were able to perform all the tasks that life imposed on us, easily solved all the problems we encountered, if we never forgot nor our memories became confused, if we were able to contain our feelings and not be corrupted by our sins, if we were immune to disease and shielded from accidents, if we never hurt nor were hurt by others, if, in short, life were only impossibly perfect!

The fact is we are not always happy or satisfied, we don't always learn easily and we are not always efficient in the way we go about our daily tasks. Our memories are not always clear. We are not always shielded from diseases nor do we contemplate accidents. Unfortunately, we do hurt others as do others hurt us.

We cannot live our lives predicated on the notion of *if only things were different or if only things were the way we wanted them to be or it won't or it can't happen to me*. Life has a big IF in the middle and this uncertainty does render us vulnerable. We have to live with the reality of how things are here and now and not with how things might, should or ought to be.

✳

Many people today expect that books such as this one will give them prescriptions on how to live their lives, or how to attain happiness or peace and sanity. It is important for you to acknowledge why you have chosen to read this book. If you are looking for answers to some very personal questions, then I am sure this book will be of assistance to you. It is important that you keep asking these questions as you continue with your reading. However, this book is not intended as a substitute for face-to-face therapy but rather as a guide.

your journey within

1
getting to know you

Together, you and I will travel through a variety of landscapes including thus far uncharted territories, vast deserts, beautiful gardens and uninhabited rainforests. We will sit behind graceful waterfalls and see splashes of water assemble to form ferocious flowing rivers.

This journey you are embarking on is a complex and changing process. It is a voyage at the end of which many people can emerge not only with an increased sense of self-awareness, assertiveness and effectiveness but also become more forthright and less inhibited. In reality, they become better equipped to take control of their lives and reach their destinations in the healthiest way possible. To illustrate, let me tell you about the parable of the *Little Stream and the Desert*.

There was once a little stream which originated after rains over far off hills. The purpose of this little stream was to overcome everything in its way and eventually reach the ocean. In its attempt to fulfil its purpose, the stream came across a desert.

Like the stream, the desert also had a purpose which was to overcome everything in its way. One day there would be a pond with shrubs and then suddenly without warning a sand storm would cover everything and the picturesque greenery would become part of the desert.

The more the tiny stream struggled to pass through the desert, the harder it became and the despairing stream found itself being absorbed into the desert. The stream was concerned that if it did not rain soon or that it was not able to cross the desert and reach the ocean, it would soon perish and not reach its destination.

The struggle left the stream, now barely a trickle, frustrated and drained. The stream was convinced that it could cross the desert, but could not see how. While the stream was struggling with the harsh environment, it heard the sound of the wind. The wind said gently: *Have faith in me and I will carry you over the desert.*

The little stream was not sure what this meant. The wind continued: *With the help of the sun you will evaporate and I will carry you over the desert and you can become rain and continue on your merry way.* The stream saw the wisdom in the wind's words but was still hesitant.

The little stream inquired: How do I know that if I rain again I will be the same stream? The wind replied: I cannot promise you that you will be the same stream, but let me ask you, would you want to be the same stream?

Do you want to be the same person at the end of your journey? Do you want to focus on the stream and miss out on everything else? After all, would this not be like getting drunk at the stream instead of being enriched by the undiluted purity at the source? More about the stream later.

You do not have to be an architect to design and build a house. If you're lucky you'll have a friend or relative who is an architect and do it for you! You most certainly don't have to be an expert on human behaviour or a behavioural scientist to live your life, but it may be helpful to know certain things about how to go about identifying and correcting your problems, if things do go wrong. This is one of the crucial issues in problem solving and even more important in understanding and untangling your inner processes.

If you have chosen to embark on this journey on your own you need faith in yourself, your abilities and you're potential to undertake the journey and, more importantly, a commitment to complete it.

Crossroads: Your Journey Within has itself emerged from a decade of hypothesising, testing, evolving and refinement. Although its origins are rooted in the classical notions of psychoanalysis, the theoretical grounding has evolved to include social, behavioural, and cognitive traditions of psychology, philosophy, sociology, metaphysics and literature.

The ideas in this book come from the science of psychotherapy. The problems examined are the issues of everyday living. The focus is you, the world within you, the people around you, the world at large. It is about how the interaction between what is inside your skin and what is outside your skin influence decisions you make, and the consequences of those decisions for yourself and those around you.

Everyone should have a near-death-like experience at least once in their lives. I don't mean that people should go out of their way and attempt to do away with themselves, wake up and lose touch with reality. I mean that everyone should have one of those out of body experiences, like in the cartoons. A chance to step outside of our bodies and look at ourselves, the way other people see us. We get so caught up in the emotional roller coaster of everyday living that we tend to lose focus of how things fit in. We tend to lose sense of the relativity of things.

There is an irony in our make-up. On the one hand we know ourselves far better than anyone else does. At least our internal prosecutor, also known as our conscience or superego, knows us better than anyone else does! On the other hand, other people are able to see us more objectively than we do through our subjective realities.

So, there you are. Standing over yourself from above and looking at yourself. What do you see? What you see is that there is somewhat of a discrepancy between who you see, who you would like to see and who you ought to see. Are you who you actually are, who other people think you ought to be or the person whom you would like to be, ideally? Looking at yourself is not simple. Nor is it easy or pain free.

Although it is important to know how other people see you, basically, you know yourself far better than anyone else does. Admitting your weaknesses and problems to yourself is like looking at yourself in a mirror. No more and no less. You can look into an image distorting mirror, but you will know that the reflection is not your true image. You may be able to convince others that the reflection is a true picture of you, but you cannot convince yourself.

This is where the journey really begins. You are left with two choices, either stop trying to convince yourself that the distorted image is real or stop denying that you are trying to convince others that your superficial facade is the real you. You get so caught up in the way you are and the way you react, that it seems to be the only way you know. In your eyes, what you do is obvious and right, and when things don't turn out as you expected you are surprised.

Until you stop just looking at the outside world and focus inside, your inner world will continue to be a rich infusion of feelings, beliefs, attitudes, dreams, fantasies and ideas, perpetuated unconsciously by the fear of what you might find and your inability to look inside and recognise the dynamics at work.

Consciously you may be aware that you often feel afraid, anxious or depressed for no apparent reason, that you find yourself repeating the same mistakes, selecting the same unsuitable people as partners or friends and still not be able to help yourself.

You may feel a sense of emptiness or lingering guilt

or self doubt and still not know why. Some of the problems such as anxiety attacks, depression, addictions, anger, low self esteem, lack of motivation, indecisiveness, sexual problems, marital problems, effects of trauma and the like, may be real or disguised and may in fact be quite debilitating for you.

Certain symptoms like depression, for example, may exist to hide deeper and more disturbing dynamics. Other symptoms such as illnesses may exist to perpetuate some secondary gain, like gaining attention from family members, exerting control or manipulating others to behave in ways that they would not otherwise behave. Remember, most of your symptoms are there for a reason. It is a fallacy to assume that if you avoid or try to escape from these intense feelings that you will be safe. Take my word for it, you will not.

Imagine a world where in the face of a crisis or a traumatic event you didn't feel shock, denial, fear, anger, anxiety or depression? What would you feel instead? The point is, if you are experiencing some undesirable feeling, you don't need to escape from that feeling. Denial, avoidance or efforts to escape don't work. There is ample evidence to suggest that if you were to sit with the feeling and try to make sense of it, you are more likely to drain the emotional energy from that feeling and actually feel self-respect for having responded rather than reacted to your feelings.

Easier said than done, you retort. Let us say that you are feeling anxious. The odds are that the anxiety that you are feeling was triggered by something you heard, said or experienced, with or without interacting with others. This is something that is occurring inside your skin and you, and only you have to deal with it. Once you have identified the triggering factors that make you feel anxious, you can then take preventative action and not expose yourself to anxiety provoking situations unnecessarily. Actions motivated by responding to an event rather than reacting have vastly different consequences. Let's not go there just yet.

The Ancient Greek Philosopher, Epictatus once advocated that; men are not disturbed by things but by their perception of things. What he didn't say was that you are ultimately responsible for how you interpret, what you interpret and what you subsequently feel or do about it. Well, you can't be any good for others if you are not being good to yourself and you can't be any good for yourself if you are not being good to others. This is clearly a process of unconditional and unequivocal reciprocation. The beauty is that you can do something about it.

The purpose of this book is not to attack the

symptoms of these debilitating problems you may be experiencing, but rather to empower you to explore the problems by focusing on the inner mechanisms at play. It is also about enabling psychological insight and the use of this insight in your day-to-day interaction with others. It is about helping you take that next step from uncertainty to stimulating an awareness.

Often gaining insight into your inner dynamics in itself may not be sufficient for you to facilitate the type of transformation sought. In fact, some difficulties are better left alone as their course of resolution may be independent of your ability to deal with them and in some cases may have very little to do with you. What is required for a break in unhealthy patterns is an actual experience of a new solution in your everyday life.

A healthy closure before a new beginning can give you the sense that a new solution is possible. By experiencing an old conflict with a healthier solution you are able to abandon your old patterns and feel free to explore healthier alternatives.

2
preparing for
your journey

To benefit from this book you will need an open mind, a preparedness to allow some of your fixed views to be scrutinised, a curiosity to explore your inner world, fantasies, dreams, thoughts, values, beliefs and a willingness to allow yourself to think, feel and experience life to create healthy dynamics.

You will also need to leave behind certain attitudes or behaviours such as the emotional weight you may have been shouldering for others. More importantly, you need to be willing, non-dismissive and patient. You need to be prepared to look into yourself, sometimes in a brutally honest fashion, and be persistent to see the journey through.

In return, you will experience change that on the surface may consist merely of a change in emphasis, but in fact is a dramatic and remarkable transformation from being unhappy, dissatisfied and drained to being focused, vibrant and creative.

Much of what you will get out of this book will depend on whether you are ready to know certain things about yourself and whether you are ready to question certain aspects of your existence that you have accepted as fact. You need to prepare for your inner journey through an awareness of the reality you experience, a self-questioning rather than a blind acceptance of basic facts and a tenacity to ask why, how and what for.

This may be difficult at first, but it will help you identify what belongs to your inner self and what belongs to the outside world. Your self-questioning, not self-doubt, will be your level of discovery towards betterment. You will need to keep it alive, like the pilot light in a gas heater.

You will need to allocate a certain amount of undistracted time for yourself. You give your time to other people. You also need some time for your-self. You may like to go for a long walk by the beach or the park once a week. This is a time to focus on your self for a change. A time to simmer in silence and to explore and reflect on your innermost thoughts and feelings.

As you continue on your journey, your self-questioning will act as your guide, and when you recall and associate past experiences with your present, your heater will turn itself on automatically but instead of heating uncontrollably, you will be in a position to adjust the heater to your needs. You will have control over whether the heater burns you or warms you up.

Let us explore the idea of having control over our lives in another dimension with a concrete analogy. The strange thing about cars is that once you purchase them and drive them out of the caryard, two things happen. The first is that they depreciate in value immediately. The second is that your car will never be the same again. If you want your car to do its job day in day out, you have to take care of it, have it serviced on time, regularly check the water levels and oil levels and make sure old parts are replaced with new ones. Otherwise, your car's engine is likely to overheat, burn oil or just break down. Just imagine that your car has broken down and you want to go forward. Now, unless you are a mechanic or have a relative who is a mechanic you will need to take your car in for repair.

The fact remains that until your car is repaired you will not be able to go forward. Being impatient, anxious, depressed or any one of the myriad of undesirable emotions, will only cause to prolong the agony for you. Your car will have to stay at the garage until the work is done.

The same applies with our emotions and interpersonal relations. If your life has been sliding backwards you will need to stop for a while until you are ready to move forward. How long you have to stop can be measured by the magnitude of the difficulties you are experiencing. This time will enable you to take stock of preceding events, define and redefine the foundations of your life domains, priorities, objectives and goals and establish new foundations. This does not mean that you have to destroy every shred of the remnants of your past, but rather throw out the unhealthy bits and retain the healthy parts of your inner and outer life as building blocks for the future.

Change in this sense is absolutely possible. You will need to start with little changes first. You may need to uncontaminate your mind from pre-meditated, impure, malicious and negative thoughts and focus on the actions that are going to best lead you to your ultimate destination. Where, when, why, how you get there are details for you to figure out.

3
fasten your seatbelts

Imagine this scene: a magician walks up to you and says to you that you are going to a deserted island for six months. The island is about a kilometre by a kilometre in size with a dozen palm trees and a few shrubs here and there. There are no books, newspapers, radios, television sets, people, animals or any other form of distraction on the island.

So that your family, friends and colleagues are not worried and unnecessarily distressed about you, the magician clones another person just like you to take your place whilst you are away. Now, you have no choice as to whether you go or not but the magician does give you a choice as to whether you go alone or take me with you. You are probably thinking: *Do I go on my own or do I go on this six-month expedition with someone I have never met?*

Make a decision as to what you are going to choose. Although some people would relish the opportunity to delve into their own little world for a few months, on the whole, most people would choose to take someone with them.

If your choice is to take me with you, then before we embark on this journey, there are certain things that I would need to know about you. For example, it would not matter to me that you had a loaded bank account, that you drove the latest model car or that you lived in a huge mansion in the best part of town.

What would matter to me is whether you were a person with integrity, honesty, consistency, compassion and empathy. Whether you were able to share your thoughts and feelings with me in a considerate and non-judgemental manner. I would want to know whether you were a worthy person.

Are you a worthy person? What this question is asking you to consider is not whether you think other people see you as a worthy person, but rather, whether you think of yourself as a worthy person. At this stage we are not concerned with what other people think of you.

If you have answered this question with a *No*, please go to the bottom of page 35 and continue reading from the paragraph beginning with an asterisk. If on the other hand, you have answered *Yes*, please read on.

Let us say that for the purposes of this exercise I believe you. Remember, I don't know you either. Now, you close your eyes and when you open your eyes again you and I will be on this deserted island. It isn't a large island where we can spend long hours exploring and discovering novel things or encountering great adventures. It is a simple island where we are totally dependent on each other to make the best of our time together.

OK. You have your little hut and I have my little hut. We don't have to worry about cooking, cleaning or our safety. That has all been taken care of. Now, how will we spend our time together? What things would you do? Would there be a routine in your daily activities or would you just simply go with the flow?

I don't know about you but I would want to communicate with you. I would want to know all about you and in return, I would want you to know all about me. I would want to know that when I was sharing my intimate thoughts and feelings with you that I had your absolute and genuine attention; sharing and communicating your real thoughts and feelings with me.

If you found me to be an honest, open, patient

and non-judgemental person, do you think that you might let me know everything there is to know about you both good and bad? Do you think that even after knowing everything about you, I might still regard you as a worthy person?

Four months have gone by and we have shared a lot without holding anything back from each other. We have shared ideas, feelings, and opinions. We have told each other stories from our travels and our past, shared funny jokes, played games, swam in the water, built sand castles, jogged on the sand, climbed the palm trees, experimented with various foods, and learnt a lot about each other and have come to respect each other's needs. In other words, we have come to enjoy each other's company and stopped chasing things that are not important.

One day I approach you and say that I would like to spend the rest of the time on the island by myself. So, I get a big stick and draw a straight line right between your hut and my hut, dividing the island into two. What do you do?

You could do a number of things. You could do nothing. If you were someone who needed to derive a sense of belonging from others, you could feel that it is your fault and retreat to your hut and exist in a state of total confusion as to what you did to cause my behaviour. You could become angry with me and retreat to your hut and contemplate ways of confronting me. You could feel disappointed about the fact that, having invited and accepted to take me with you, I have rejected you. You could throw the stick at me!

You could accept my need for privacy and let me be or you could approach me and try to communicate with me to clarify why, having agreed to come with you on this six-month journey and thus far having allowed such intimacy to develop, I have chosen to withdraw from you.

How you perceive yourself will affect what you think, feel and do, which will ultimately determine the consequences of your actions.

The difference between a healthy and an unhealthy choice is that an unhealthy choice stems from a mind that operates in a way that is a repetition of the same past choices. When certain factors such as situation, time and people, get together, the person thinks, feels and behaves in a programmed manner. A healthy choice on the other hand, eventuates from a mind that is able to consider the dynamics of all the possible options and decides on the one that leads to the healthiest possible outcome.

Imagine that you have just come home. You have

been living with your partner for about two years. From your point of view your relationship is quite a happy one. You get to the door and find a note. It reads: *It has been great knowing you, but I have gone off with your best friend.*

Now, if your tendency is to blame yourself, you may say to yourself: *My partner was a great person, I do not think that I can find another partner like him or her*. You may then proceed to drink your self silly and go for that fatal drive in your car to express your anger by being self-destructive.

Same scene. You have just arrived home and find the same note at the door. If your tendency is to think about your options first, you might instead say to yourself: *My partner was a great person, but I tried everything possible to make the relationship work and if he or she cannot appreciate this, then it is their loss.* You may feel sad that the relationship has ended, but you can look forward to another relationship so you do not make the same mistakes again.

If you have been able to follow so far, we are on track.

Now, what of people who chose to go alone? If you have chosen to go on this six-month journey alone, it is important that you understand your reasons for wanting to go alone.

If you are delighted at the opportunity to spend six months away from the complexity of everyday living, if you are challenged, if you are curious about your ability to cope on your own, if you would rather not spend six months with a stranger, whom you have never met or will never meet or any one of several reasons which do not involve avoidance, denial or an indication of interpersonal difficulty, please enjoy your six-month holiday.

However, if you feel that you have difficulty defining boundaries, controlling your aggression, anger, hostility, depression, feelings of homicide or suicide or find close relationships threatening you should stop reading this book and seek professional assistance immediately! Now, close your eyes and when you open them again you will find yourself sitting in front of a therapist.

4

the road to the self

Understanding your self is complex. Let us begin with the notion that the self is made up of a number of dimensions. The dimension of *tangible self* is that part of us that is observable, measurable and touchable. The dimension of *conditional self* consists of what other people think our *self* ought to be. Then there is the dimension of *unconditional self*, which consists of who we would ultimately like to be. Finally, there is the dimension that consists of all the things about our self that we don't like. Our internal prosecutor regulates the interaction between these dimensions. To complicate matters further, the combination of these dimensions forms the self which exists within the dimensions of thoughts, feelings and actions. Most people think happy thoughts, feel happy feelings and do happy things. However, we are not always this consistent. Sometimes we have unhappy thoughts, feel unhappy feelings and do unhappy things.

Let us imagine that you and I have been friends for the past ten years. In that time we have come to share a great deal and know each other quite well. Imagine that four weeks ago you met this person and you would like to introduce that person to me. However, before I meet this person, I ask you to describe this person to me. This person is you.

Now, how would you describe this person? Is this person friendly, honest, reliable, trustworthy, caring and unpretentious? Is this person able to take responsibility for his or her actions? Is this person consistent in their intentions and actions? Is this person able to make a commitment to a friendship and is considerate of other's needs? Is it important for this person to nurture close and meaningful friendships? Is this person able to give and take and not play manipulative emotional games? These qualities are important to me and I would like to know the answers to some of these questions, before I meet this person. Do you nurture these qualities?

5
meet your internal prosecutor

This is a good time to introduce a third party to this scenario. Your Internal Prosecutor. My what? You might ask. Your internal prosecutor is your conscience. It is that little voice inside your mind that tries to and sometimes succeeds in differentiating between good and bad. Our conscience is part of an intricate psychological web that controls our sense of right or wrong, appropriate or inappropriate, ethical or unethical, moral or immoral, healthy or unhealthy, balanced or unbalanced and the like.

We are born with a set of drives that are beyond our control. Hunger, thirst, aggression and the like. At some point, the expression of these drives is not conducive to our smooth interaction with others. Therefore, our superego which is an identification and internalisation of parental and social conditioning, regulates our drives in the form of reality testing and constraint. Our ego is that part of us that acts as a buffer between our basic drives and the parental and social imperatives. A healthy internal prosecutor demands that there is some consistency and balance between our drives and the reality of parental and social conditioning and restraint.

Most of the time, the internal prosecutor is just there, perpetually lying half asleep deep within you. Often pretending to be asleep, it is just waiting for the opportunity to examine and cross-examine you. Waiting vigilantly to attack your defences.

Next time something bad happens to you, just observe. The first attack on you is by your internal prosecutor. What you need to appreciate is that your internal prosecutor is like a good friend who is playing the devil's advocate. It has your best interests at heart. Next time you hear a faint voice from within you assessing the ethics of your thoughts, feelings and behaviour, listen to your internal prosecutor but ask, so what? Do not over-rule the objection when it should be sustained.

Your internal prosecutor knows everything about you. It knows every little sin, every feeling, thought or action that you have ever experienced and tried to hide away. It knows about all of your emotional, financial, social, and personal failures. All the times you were rejected by others, especially the opposite sex. All the secret thoughts that you have been afraid to share with anyone.

If you let it, your internal prosecutor will use these against you. It is your task to remind your internal prosecutor of your successes, achievements and positive qualities. Whatever accusations are thrown at you, these are not aimed at weakening your defences, but rather to help you assess the choices you are making; in order that you make the healthiest choices.

I live close to a major road which is crowded with shops of various sorts. The fashion shops are my favourites. Not because I purchase my clothes from them, but because I find such a parallel between these shops and people. Often, these shops have window displays for people like me to do our seasonal window-shopping. The display clothes are usually arranged in such a way that some of the more attractive and appealing clothes are displayed with reasonable prices, along with the ordinary ones.

Now, if you find yourself being pulled into one of these shops, you often find that not all the clothes are of good quality and not all are reasonably priced. It is the same with people. Not all is as it first appears. First impressions can sometimes be misleading. Whether it be consciously or unconsciously, you often end up finding yourself behaving in ways that are directed at particular objectives. For example, distancing as a way of keeping people at bay because you are afraid of close relationships. Distancing is the means to another end, which in this case, might be to protect yourself from being hurt by others. The difficulty is if you remain distant from others. Yes, you may protect yourself, but you also miss out on the richness that close relationships can bring.

We do and say things to please others, to maintain our distance, to acquire certain things or because we lack the basic skills to make demands of our own. Consequently, we allow others to see only those aspects of our personality that we have control over and think is acceptable. However, given the fact that ways of avoiding our painful feelings can be more destructive or painful in themselves, we are concerned with what you do to avoid anger, pain, depression, conflict and the ways you attempt to control unacceptable feelings.

We do not want others, and sometimes ourselves, to see what is beyond our own window display. We employ all sorts of devices to achieve this. We are afraid that if others see inside, they might not like what they see.

So you continue to exist in a constant state of

stand-by as if you are going to be found out any second. Occasionally, you let someone in, only to find that your fears are confirmed. So you ask yourself, *why do people do this to me?* Others ask, *why do I let people do this to me?* Some go further and ask, *Why am I like this?*

How many times have you asked yourself one or all of these questions? Too often? Well, the point at which you start consciously asking these questions, with an obvious need to find the answers is also the point at which you need to become aware that this is not the first time you have asked these questions. This is also the point at which the process of tracing these questions back to their source begins.

When we take a good look at ourselves, we find that we all hold many beliefs that we don't even agree with. Since these beliefs, values, expectations and attitudes determine to a large extent the choices we make and how we live our lives, they have an impact on our happiness in a very powerful way.

So, what should you do? You already know what to do but you have difficulty doing it. You just need to understand the forces operating in you that prevent you from doing exactly what it is that you want to do.

Due to your own specific reasons, you are unable to bring into your conscious reality the mechanisms that prevent you from achieving your full potential.

This leads to all sorts of problems, such as frustration, guilt, anger, depression, withdrawal and the like. The unconscious mechanisms often cause tension both within yourself and in your interactions with other people.

Because you are still not aware of your own inner mechanisms, you internalise the problems through your destructive and self-reproaching inner dialogue. The futile cycle is not broken and you continue to exist in this vicious misery-go-round.

When you internalise external problems such as going along with others about an issue which you have strong or a conflicting opinion about, what you are actually doing is awakening your internal prosecutor who is always gathering evidence and is ready to judge and punish you for your shortcomings, on the spot. This mechanism, once triggered, sets in motion a complex psychological aggression against yourself.

This is an important mechanism that needs elaboration and understanding. Armed with this knowledge, you could avoid unnecessary pain and suffering.

Many of the unfortunate situations you have experienced or will experience in the future, have similar features. The consequent confusion and pain you feel is often out of proportion to the situation that confronts you. The pain often persists far beyond the duration of the original experience. Sometimes days, weeks, months and in some cases years after the experience, the pain lingers on. Some people get stuck and eventually find themselves feeling that life is not worthwhile. Without sounding like a moral or religious dogmatic, you did not give yourself life and you have no right to end it. No matter how overwhelming life gets, it is better to live.

Regardless, you feel taxed far beyond your emotional capacity. You feel increasing resentment towards others, especially those around you. So, what can you do differently to avoid the pain, suffering and loss that you and those around you are vulnerable to?

If the situation warrants it, accept responsibility for your faults. Admit that you have screwed up. Accept that it is your fault. So what? How important is this in the grand scheme of things? The solution is not in conducting a witchhunt to find someone to blame, but rather to focus on what to do about the problem. Do not attempt to argue with your internal prosecutor about who is to blame for the situation. This only serves to distract you from the real objective, which is to solve the problem.

It is interesting to note that arguments between people follow the same dynamic as arguments between you and your internal prosecutor. Notice how when something goes wrong or when conflict occurs, wives, husbands, fathers, teachers, bosses and almost everyone else you interact with, are ready to launch an attack on you based on the notion that it is all your fault!

Your internal prosecutor sets the dynamic for the outer prosecutors to point the finger at you. What you have to understand is that everyone around you also has an internal prosecutor, unrelentingly accusing and attacking them. They are merely following directions from their own internal prosecutor who is defending itself from possible guilt and defensively pointing at you.

Where do you think the concept of *defensiveness* comes from? No one likes to accept blame for failure. So, to defend themselves from the knowledge of having failed, people often just deny their own responsibility and project outwards by pointing the finger at others.

Pointing the finger at yourself or others, instead of focusing on ways of resolving conflict or dealing with failure, is often only a partial solution. Your internal prosecutor takes note of this denial and saves it for a rainy day. When a situation recurs sometime in the future, your internal prosecutor uses the information against you, when you least expect it. How much longer can you continue to blame yourself or others?

We are more ready to accept responsibility when we succeed. It is easier for us to accuse and blame others for our failures. Once you understand this, your life will become much easier and your interaction with others, much smoother. You will be able to anticipate who is going to attack you when things do go wrong. You also need to become aware of your own internal prosecutor and anticipate his line of attack. You can achieve this by becoming aware of how you empower your internal prosecutor in the first place.

What is he talking about? If this question has anchored in your mind, let me demonstrate.

There was once a little man who lived in a little house. One day he decided that he wanted to go on a little journey. He packed his little bag and headed for the door. He locked his door and was just about to leave the front gate when his neighbour, who saw him leaving approached him and asked: *Where are you going?*
The little man explained that he was going on a little journey.
His neighbour asked: *You mean, you are going on a little journey God willing.*
The little man replied: *No, I am going on a journey.*

As soon as he said this he was turned into a little green frog and placed in a frog pond where he lived the life of a little green frog for seven years.

At the end of the seventh year he was turned back into a little man again. The little man rushed to his little house, packed his little bag and once again headed for the door. He was about to leave his house when the same neighbour approached him again.

The neighbour asked: *Where are you going?*

The little man again explained that he was going on a little journey.

His neighbour asked: *You mean, you are going on a little journey, God willing?*

The little man replied: *No, I am going on a little journey or back to the frog pond!*

When the little man became aware of the only realistic option open to him through trial and error, he was no longer the same man who was oblivious to reality. He realised and accepted that if he did not seek God's blessing to go on the little journey, he would end up in the frog pond again.

God willing, do you wish to continue on your journey or go back to the frog pond?

6
the road home

There are stages in your life where certain natural and irreversible transformations have already taken place. These are beyond your control. For example, the transitions from childhood to adolescence and subsequently from adolescence to adulthood are probably the greatest of the transformations.

This footbridge which eventually leads you to maturity involves an exponential growth in your thoughts, feelings, attitudes and actions, and is invariably beyond your conscious control. What happens to you during these stages may not be in your control, yet has a significant impact on your development. When you were a newborn baby, you had a mass of needs. You needed to be held, kept warm, cleaned, fed, protected and loved. You were entirely dependent on those around you to satisfy your needs. At this stage of your development, you were unable to perceive the needs of others, let alone meet them.

The most significant thing you could give to others was the satisfaction of being seen to respond to the care you were given. These early experiences are absorbed and stored inside by your internal prosecutor. We call this learning. More precisely, learning to recognise your place in your environment. Although we never really stop learning, once the basic foundation is formed, it becomes the frame of reference through which we view the world.

Unfortunately, due to early extreme deprivation, poverty, loss and alienation coupled with an unhealthy environment, some people carry this inside them without realising the damaging consequences. These people tend to contaminate healthy experiences and have difficulty containing happy and uplifting feelings.

Through socialisation, education and work, we learn to modify and build on the foundations to keep us up to date with the changing environmental conditions. However, when you go through the processes of socialisation, education and cultural conditioning, grow up and become an adult, you are expected to put a large part of your own needs aside and take responsibility for those of others.

Very few of us are taught how to reconcile the massive changes in the expectations imposed on us and, as a consequence, suffer. We are left to our own devices and eventually, through trial and error and in some cases pure chance, learn to achieve a balance between satisfying our own needs and satisfying the needs of others. Or do we?

We need to understand how this transition impacts on us. How this transition is effected will have a significant bearing on your development.

Firstly, you must be given enough to meet your needs sufficiently. Otherwise, you may find it difficult to give to others, especially those close to you, what you yourself need.

You may defensively and compulsively give to others and resent them for the emotional deficit that you feel due to the fact that your giving has not been reciprocated. This may lead to you having difficulty with giving and receiving in your interactions. Some people equate neediness with weakness. So, they try all sorts of tactics to hide their neediness. They are ready and eager to give to others. Unfortunately, this often leads to interpersonal breakdown. By not allowing natural expression of neediness by making reasonable demands on others, they create the impression that they can cope with any crisis. This leads others to experience them as strong and not in need. Others feel that they have not been permitted to reciprocate in kind. Neediness is not a weakness.

Secondly, you need to be guided gently and firmly into the knowledge that not all of your demands can be met and that others have needs, as well as you. Your needs are important. However, other people's needs are equally as important.

Not having your demands met may be experienced by you as a deprivation, which it is. If this requirement is carried out too slowly or not at all, you are likely to become selfish and spoiled and unable to tolerate frustration and the demands of others.

If you do not receive enough to satisfy your developmental needs, or if your personal needs are not acknowledged, you may feel genuinely deprived, resentful that your needs are not met and experience difficulty tolerating other people's demands on you and in turn disappoint them.

Teresa's Story

Teresa was one of those unfortunate people who never found her way home. A place where she could be herself. A place where she felt safe and secure. Over the years, a desperate feeling of not belonging anywhere left a permanent *lost* expression on her face. Like the expression on the face of a traveller lost in a foreign country; unable to speak the language and ask for help or relate to anyone. She was afraid of being hurt and suspicious of everything and everyone, like a boat without a helm, rudder or anchor.

Teresa's father left her mother soon after Teresa was born. She had no contact with her father. Teresa spent her entire life seeking her father in other men. She was forty seven when she acknowledged this fact.

Until she was ten, her mother was the only person who was allowed into her small world. Then, her mother remarried and Teresa lived with her mother and stepfather for the next five years. Teresa felt betrayed by her mother and lived in constant fear of losing her.

Her stepfather was a cold and cruel man who showed no reason or warmth. The situation became desperate and hopeless when he lost his job and began spending long hours at home, in a drunken state. Taking opportunity of his wife's trust and a little defenceless child's innocence, he grabbed her by the hair and dragged her into a crazy world where there were no rules.

When Teresa turned fifteen, her mother died of cancer. Her world fell apart. The one person, who was her anchor in life, had died and her grief was beyond words. She sought comfort from her grief in her stepfather who had other things on his mind and seemed sadistically cheerful about his wife's death. Teresa was determined to disappear at the first opportunity.

Three months after her mother died, Teresa found out that she was pregnant. To her shock, her stepfather threw her out of the house. With little money and nowhere to go, she found herself living in a boarding house frequented by hardened criminals and drug pushers. Here, she managed to befriend Bertie.

Bertie, although fond of Teresa, seemed incapable of looking after himself, let alone a pregnant girlfriend. She did not care. At least, she thought, he cares about me. Teresa managed to convince Bertie that she was pregnant to him. This newfound responsibility triggered Bertie to do something about the miserable conditions of their existence.

After several unsuccessful attempts at finding a job, Bertie managed to secure a job working in a butcher store. Soon after, they managed to move into a small apartment and get married. For the first time in her life, Teresa felt happy.

Teresa and Bertie remained together for the next twenty-two years and had four more children.

With the passing years, Teresa's feeling of

achievement and happiness became increasingly confused by her feelings of emptiness, resentment and restlessness. Her marriage was a stormy relationship, full of sporadic episodes of brutality and violence. Teresa was beginning to feel that she had nothing left to give to her family. She spent most of her adult life giving to her husband and her children a sense of belonging, but kept her own need for a sense of belonging at bay.

On the eve of her thirty-ninth birthday, a climactic event occurred. Teresa had gone shopping with the children and on her return, found her stepfather and her husband sitting in the kitchen and talking about her.

Bertie had found out that he was not the father of the first child and was building up a storm. Her stepfather left as soon as Teresa arrived. Teresa feared the worst. Suddenly she was reminded of her painful past. She dropped the shopping, grabbed the car keys and left.

She drove for hours, directionless and with one single thought going over and over in her mind. Enough! She did not know whether she was running away from her family or herself.

A week later, having nowhere to go, Teresa found herself standing at her front door trying to decide whether she was going to walk in or walk away. She was uncertain. She felt that she did not belong there yet at the same time, knew that this was her house, her children and her husband. For the first time, Teresa was confronted with having to find some realistic compromise, a balance, between her need for a sense of belonging and putting her own needs aside and giving to those around her.

Our natural tendency to reciprocate can sometimes become distorted. We can suffer by not allowing others to give back in their own unique way because of our own confusion about weakness. This can often make things more complicated than they need to be.

7
the road from depression

So you are feeling depressed? Sorry, I can't help you. Hang on a minute! I know someone who can help you though. Would you like to meet that person? I will guide you to that person, but you have to follow the directions carefully. Step by step.

Step 1   Hold this book open in your right hand.

Step 2   Walk to the bathroom.

Step 3   Close the door behind you.

Step 4   Look around and find the mirror.

Step 5   Stand in front of the mirror.

Step 6   Close your eyes and count to 10.

Step 7   Open your eyes.

Now, who do you see? Let me introduce you to the person who wants you to be depressed. Meet YOU.

You see, reactive depression, which is a type of depression resulting from your reaction to certain events, is something that is transient, caused by an inability to deal with overwhelming external stresses such as a demotion or interpersonal conflict, and, unless you want to be depressed and hang on to it, it will go away. Let me rephrase that. Unless you want to be depressed your depression will go away. Most of your depression is caused by the irrational things you tell yourself about what you fear or expect might happen to you. Who says? Where is the evidence? The odds are that it won't.

People who experience frequent episodes of depression have certain features in common. Firstly, they expect the worst of every situation. The reality is that most of the time, the things that they feel so depressed about, the imminent disasters that they fear so much, never occur.

Secondly, they have various beliefs that maintain and perpetuate their depression. They believe that they should be happy all the time, that the world should be fair and just, that their future is determined by their past and that they have no control over what happens to them. And because of these beliefs, they have unrealistic expectations of others and a distorted view of the world.

Thirdly, these people have a tendency to see things totally out of proportion. They tend to magnify and exaggerate the smallest of mishaps into huge catastrophes.

Fourthly, some people have a tendency to cope with criticism, conflict or adverse situations by attempting to avoid these situations. However, when problems do occur, they react by denying the importance, the future implications, their responsibility and contribution to the problem they are facing. This is perhaps one way of explaining how people get depressed. If you do share some of the blame, then take responsibility for it. The worse thing you could do for yourself is denial.

Denial is your internal prosecutor's best weapon against you. When he lets the floodgates of depression open with his accusations, you have an unbearably heavy weight pressing you down because you are defenceless against his indisputable accusations.

Have you noticed I have not explored guilt? Pretty depressing, I would say. But, as sad as it is, people who have a tendency for depression also feel guilt. About everything! Can it be because guilt is related to denial?

The good news is that there is hope. There is ample clinical evidence to suggest that if you did do nothing, your depression will subside. With a little help, it might go away altogether. Now, try to think back and pinpoint the exact thought that triggered the depressing feeling in you. What was it? Was it something you heard? Something an important friend pointed out? Something that reminded you of your past that you have been hiding from yourself? The moment you become aware of what you have been telling yourself about what happened, ask yourself: *So what?*

Now, stop whatever you have been doing and undertake something physical. Go for a run or a swim. Chop some wood or do some gardening. You see depression hates physical activity and by the time you are finished, you can almost be sure that your depression will have subsided.

Remember, depression is there to distract you from the real problems that threaten you. It is one of many weapons available to your internal prosecutor to render you helpless. Are you going to let him win one over you? Depression does not have to be part of your life, if you don't want it to be.

Most depressed people have someone around them. Those who have no one are most vulnerable to a chronic form of depression, which is more intractable and needs professional attention. Crucially so, as isolation from others appears to significantly influence the frequency and duration of the depression.

To understand depression at a deeper level, we need to focus on a number of golden rules. These rules dictate the manner and nature of the professional work in mental health. These rules also apply when looking at depression. Depression is every professional therapists pet disorder, at least to begin with. There are over a dozen different explanations, theories and views regarding the causes of depression.

We know that virtually anything can trigger it. When it comes to assessing and treating depression, there are just as many purported remedies. It seems that what works for one person may not be an accurate predictor of what works for others. Suffice to say, each person tends to experience depression in their own way and recover from depression at their own pace

In reality, it is not as clear-cut. Very few people experience depression only. Most people struggle to contain their guilt, anger, fear, and despair, sometimes intricately fused together in different combinations under the guise of depression. Often they are severely incapacitated and powerless because whatever is overwhelming them is far more than they can accommodate.

If a person is physically exhausted, emotionally challenged, spiritually drained and has no defences left to cope, then, you would naturally expect their entire being to shut down. For how long they shut down will depend on a number of things. Some of the factors include whether or not they had experienced depression previously, and if so, for what duration and how did they cope? Lack of inner resources and the acute nature of the preceding events and triggers have been found to significantly prolong depression. In addition, the lack of positive regard from others and gradual alienation from the ideal self as well as isolation from others have also been found to be significant contributors.

More often than not, depression lifts when the conditions around us improve.

8

the road from conflict

There are several types of conflict available depending on your taste. There is the conflict that stems from having to make a choice between two equally attractive options that for one reason or another are difficult to pursue at the same time.

Do you eat out Italian or Indian tonight? Do you wear jeans and a t-shirt or a suit? Do you have your hair cut long or short? These conflict situations are a common occurrence in everyday life and are of the least concern. This is because once you start focusing on which option to pursue and consider the positive aspects of that option, the alternative becomes less appealing and the conflict is easily resolved.

There is conflict that generates from confronting two equally unattractive options, where the avoidance of one means experiencing the other. They are therefore mutually exclusive. A person who suffers from dentist phobia and yet at the same time has a chronic toothache, will find him or herself in this unenviable conflict situation.

Such situations are difficult to resolve and produce significant stress, not only because the solution requires exposure to an aversive situation but also because these situations are unavoidable.

Then there is conflict where one option has both attractive and unattractive features. A child who enjoys ice-cream and is told that he cannot have ice-cream for dessert until he has finished his vegetables, faces this conflict. In this situation, the experiencing of positive features also requires the exposure to the aversive aspects and the avoidance of the undesirable features requires the giving up of the positive aspects. Unless you can, with a bit of creativity, make it all worthwhile. In our household we have a long standing rule: *If you cook you don't wash.* I love cooking. Truth be known, I also don't mind doing the dishes. Let's not get side tracked...

The ultimate consequence for someone exposed to this type of conflict situation is alternation between confronting and avoiding the situation which generates significant negative feelings such as resentment, anger, indecisiveness and low self esteem.

As far as conflict in our daily lives is concerned, we are interested in difficult situations which inherently contain conflict of the kind where choosing one option is at the expense of another, and the options are mutually exclusive.

The conflict between your needs and other people's demands on you is one such context which may have far reaching consequences for you. As an adult you might ask: *Well is it not better for me to be on my own because the problems associated with being with other people is just not worth the effort?*

Anna's Story

Anna asked herself the same question at the age of twenty-nine. For six months she had avoided becoming involved with other people by keeping her relationships as superficial as possible.

She made sure that she only saw her friends during work hours, kept contact to a minimum and only by talking on the telephone. She went out once or twice a month, often just to see a play with a friend and never got emotionally involved. Although this helped her better her career as a lawyer, it was far from sufficient to compensate for her feelings of loneliness, isolation and superficiality.

Whenever her relationships, with the same or

opposite sex, got below the level of superficiality, Anna felt afraid of her vulnerability, neediness, the primitive nature of her feelings and most importantly, of losing control. Anna wasn't always like this. During her early childhood her parents were absent for a lot of the time because of having to go to work. Anna was often left with relatives or her mother's friends.

Over the years, Anna came to see herself as a rejected child with a sense of not belonging anywhere. Her parent's lack of insight into Anna's emotional needs, evidenced by their attempt to substitute material objects for emotional nurturing, only served to cement her feelings.

During her second year at university, Anna became involved in her first serious relationship with an older man who was completing a doctoral dissertation in political sociology. Three months into the relationship they began living together and soon after married.

Although Anna felt it was all a bit too quick, she found comfort in the feeling of belonging. However, due to her husband's lecturing, travelling and study commitments, Anna found herself spending most of her time at home by herself.

Brushing her long red hair to the side, Anna revealed the core of her emotional turmoil. In every other way Anna's life was perfect Yet she was somehow unsettled. She said that having not only felt being unwanted but also having experienced it most of her life, she now felt a sense of peace and relief. It is better to feel the grief of being rejected and unwanted than to maintain false feelings. It is better to be jolted by love and hate than to exclude yourself from all relationships, without which you can never receive anything of worth or meaning.

Unable to communicate her feelings to her husband and again feeling unwanted, Anna became increasingly withdrawn and resentful. Anna was far from ready to hear herself. This pattern continued for the next six years, until she decided to leave her husband.

At the age of twenty-nine Anna began working in a large law firm. Although she found her work very demanding, she found it difficult to express her needs and ask for assistance for fear of rejection. Her colleagues saw her as being fiercely independent and in control and left her alone.

Three jobs and five relationships later, Anna found herself heading for a major breakdown. She didn't want to be alone and she couldn't risk another relationship. This conflict situation is difficult to resolve.

However, like Anna, it's not that you would rather be on your own, it's that you feel that when things don't go the way you want them to, you have no other choice and you are stuck between the two mutually exclusive alternatives.

When you are emotionally driven and forced to make contact with others, because of your inner beliefs about who you are, the way you see others becomes distorted. You do not know what you are expected to say and do and because you do not know yourself, you appear actually selfish, controlling and distant and tend to get left alone as a consequence. Your inner conflict becomes obviously manifest in your daily interactions with others.

This is the opposite of what you want and you suffer because you are not developing the skills for meeting and talking to people. Skills such as expressing your emotions appropriately, getting in touch with your experiences so you are able to take control of your life, your ability to make a difference in your environment, recognising that no matter what happens, you have the basic right to happiness, and getting in touch with the love you feel and are able to offer others.

There are some skills that you may need to learn to improve your self-confidence and break the cycle. What I'm saying is that, as a starting point, there is no useful point in trying to control what is happening outside you skin, most of which you don't have control over anyway. However, you do have control over what is happening inside your skin. More precisely, inside your mind and heart and spirit. If you are a victim, then you are likely to create a world inside your skin that either perpetuates the victim or builds defences to make sure you are not victimised. Most of us are somewhere in between the two. The beauty of it is that you can have absolute control over what is happening inside your skin.

The fact that you are not familiar with appropriate conflict resolution and assertive communication skills to mediate your interaction with others, when combined with your inner negative dialogue, only confirms your beliefs and alienates you from others even further. Contrary to the rhetoric of conflict, in real life there are only two types of conflict: destructive and constructive conflict. Whereas the former is undesirable and negative, the latter is often desirable and positive as it generates reparation, growth and life satisfaction.

9

the road from self destruction

A tendency for self destructiveness is a form of escape. It is an escape from responsibility, growing up and reality. It originates from a need to eliminate inner powerlessness and alienation. Often, self-destructive behaviour results in powerlessness, alienation, and a lot of pain and loss.

When we look around us, it is difficult not to be overwhelmed by the amount of destructiveness that exists. A destructive tendency that is a reaction to attacks on our integrity and our life can be viewed as a natural and necessary aggression that is an essential survival skill.

In this chapter, we are not concerned with this type of rational destructiveness. Our focus is on another type of destructive tendency that is irrational, inappropriate and defies our natural inclination for self-preservation. This type of destructiveness, which is directed at the self, exists within the person and is constantly waiting for the right opportunity to be expressed.

When the self becomes the object of irrational destructive impulses, severe consequences such as physical illness, emotional disturbances, poverty and even suicidal or homicidal behaviour may ensue.

Certain type of behaviours which ultimately lead to self-destruction, result from the overwhelming constraints imposed on us. If we feel powerless to overcome these constraints then we are more likely to direct our energies towards self destruction.

Addictions, for example, and more specifically pathological gambling behaviour, are one such example of self-destruction.

To understand the magnitude of the complexity of a pathological gambler's mind, we need to ask two questions relating to the motivation and the basic need that is being fulfilled by gambling. What is the motive of the pathological gambler? Answering this question will inevitably lead to our understanding of their need. More specifically, what powerful need does a pathological gambler have, that is not being satisfied and is maintaining the self-destructive behaviour?

The answer to this question needs a little more elaboration. A need is a requirement and a motive is the desire to satisfy that need. In looking at the evidence for these questions, we rely on the clinical profiles of more than eighty pathological gamblers. The trends among this specific group of pathological gamblers are evidenced by several important hallmarks that serve to distinguish this group from others. These include compulsive and pathological behaviour in the face of repeated loss; depleting own and close family member's financial resources through their compulsion and the experience of the compulsion, guilt, depression, anger, self-reproach, denial and compulsion cycle. Lack of any interest in social activities and previously enjoyed activities such as work and sport, and a tendency towards social isolation, significantly reduced communication with others, including family members, and an obsession with satisfying their compulsion, such as finding money to continue gambling.

Other characteristics include a desensitisation to loss and an apparent lack of any direction regarding work, family, relationships and goals, both intra and interpersonally. There is also an apparent and compulsive need to habitually obtain from the immediate environment a reward, which on the surface appears to be fulfilling a fundamental need for the gambler but which, on closer examination, appears to be no more than a self-destructive mechanism. For example, one patient reported drinking 38 cans of beer in two days and smoking two packets of cigarettes a day, indicating a tendency for multiple-addictions. The gamblers also displayed an apparent lack of any giving or the prolonged experience of withholding from parents or significant others during the formative years of the gambler; and the lack of any giving, or withholding due to the absence of one or both parents due to death or marital separation.

The logical conclusion from these set of observations is that for a specific group of pathological gamblers who can be identified by the above hallmarks, gambling is merely another mechanism whereby they attempt to fulfil a need through their struggle to acquire from their environment what they intrinsically feel has been withheld from them. The underlying severity of the deprivation can be measured by the intensity of the compulsion to gamble and the extent of self destruction that ensues from repeated losses. The manifest intensity of the pathology can be measured by the discrepancy in the gambler's lifestyle both before and after prolonged compulsive gambling behaviour.

The fact that there is very little focus on winning or

losing (these gamblers continue gambling, even if they have won significant amounts of money, only to lose it) and that they seek help only when the loss becomes overwhelming for them, is indicative of their attempt to gain control over the deprivation experienced by trying to obtain what is withheld from them. An appropriate analogy might be some- one who is hungry and in an attempt to fulfil their hunger, drinks a glass of water, only to find that they are still hungry.

Suicide is the ultimate form of self-destructiveness. Unable to control his environment, feeling powerless to effect change and having no sense of maintaining contact with reality, he threatens to take his own life. Not because he wants to end his life but because, at that moment, life and death are the only two things he has control over. If he chooses to exercise that control, he will take his own life and maybe the lives of others. If he chooses not to exercise that control, then he is rendered socially impotent. This is the motivation that leads him to consider the serious possibility of suicide in the first place.

To understand life we need to look back into our past. To live life we need to look into the future. Somewhere between understanding life and actually living life we are continuously at crossroads. We bring everything that we are to these crossroads. Imagine thousands of people at crossroads both within themselves and on the outside. The choices we make determine which paths we take. If we choose self-destructive paths, we will soon find ourselves isolated.

People who self preserve as opposed to self-destruct demonstrate qualities that are distinctive. They are purposeful in their self-preservation. They are not selfish. They are in harmony with the world they live in, they need peace and stability and they strive to achieve a balance in their lives. These people are builders not destroyers. They are inclusive and not exclusive. They strive to reach a balance as consumers and as producers. They also respect the collective need to survive which requires their conformity to collective rules. You can't afford to be self-destructive if you respect life and our collective need to survive.

10

the road to emotional freedom

You meet someone. For the first few days, weeks, maybe even months, you are lost in the novelty of it all; only to find that your deepest feelings of excitement, togetherness and lovingness creeps to the surface. This is natural. As you continue to exchange feelings, thoughts and actions and reveal the real you, you gradually allow your defences to be exposed as well. If you have been unable to overcome the power struggle that inevitably ensues, you are likely to experience turbulent and troublesome interpersonal relations.

When you are open and upfront with people you may become fearful because you are also exposed to being hurt. When your feelings are threatened in any way you are pulled back to your past feelings of insecurity, grief, hurt, rejection, and the like. You retreat and prepare for the worst. This is what fear does to you.

By exploring and experiencing constructive ways of expressing your feelings, you may be able to prevent yourself from being isolated. It is important that you learn clean and constructive ways of fighting rather than the dirty and destructive arguments which tend to cause rifts, are damaging and often impossible to mend.

There are many distinctive ways of dealing with inevitable arguments which may assist you to achieve closeness rather than distance.

Constructive expression of feelings places a specific negative overtone within a broad positive undertone. For example, rather than saying to your partner: you are stupid, you could state that what your partner did at that moment was a stupid thing to do. This does not carry the condemnatory emphasis and will enable your partner to save face; at the same time giving your partner an opportunity to change his or her ways.

Another way of nurturing cooperation is by volunteering praise and acceptance and expressing warmth and love. For example, volunteering to a friend that your friendship is important to you, can go a long way in expressing your desire that the relationship continue and grow.

This is not as easy as it sounds. Getting in touch with and expressing our true feelings is difficult, especially if they are painful. The tendency, perhaps in reaction to this, is to bottle our feelings inside because we do not know what else to do with them. We often don't like what we feel inside and consequently we don't like ourselves because we have these feelings.

We carry these bottled up feelings with us where ever we go. Sometimes we catch ourselves feeling depressed, miserable, anxious and lonely for no obvious reason. Sometimes we find ourselves crying at something apparently insignificant on the news or in a movie and not know why.

Jack's Story

Jack started to look at his life closely when he realised that he found it difficult to accept things from others in spite of the fact that he spent most of his adult life caring for and giving to others. Jack was separated from his father at the age of ten when his mother decided to end years of abuse and along with her three children left her husband.

In spite of an absent father, Jack lived a reasonably healthy life. However, he could not understand why his mother had decided to leave his father. Jack missed his father but could not share these feelings with his mother or anyone else.

Ten years later he received a phone call from the local police who asked him to come and identify his father who had been found dead in a hotel nearby. Jack had not seen his father since the separation and found the whole experience quite disturbing.

When Jack turned twenty-one, his mother gave him a watch. She made it well known that she had worked very hard to pay for the watch and constantly reminded him of this. Jack came to not only dislike the watch but also his mother. This resentment gradually turned into hatred. Jack felt that he could never please his mother no matter what he did. For years he kept his feelings to himself but at the same time put his own needs aside to look after his mother.

Eventually, Jack married and moved away from his mother. He became quite a successful businessman. He felt he had everything he could ever ask for. The only problem was that he felt this lingering feeling of emptiness inside. Unable to express his own needs, he went out of his way to please his wife. The more he gave to his wife, the more he resented her because he felt that he could not please her. After ten years of marriage he left his wife.

For the next two years Jack lived a desperate life. He began drinking copiously and started experimenting with hard drugs. He lost his business and not long after found himself seriously thinking about suicide.

In the midst of his own crisis, Jack found out that his mother had developed cancer and was at her deathbed. When he heard the news of his mother's condition, Jack felt a sense of retribution which gave him pleasure. Then guilt followed.

Sitting opposite me, Jack was finding it difficult to articulate what he was feeling and contemplating. His feelings were intense, confusing and uncomfortable for him. He was feeling love, hate, anger, grief, guilt, retribution and pleasure. All directed at one person, his mother. This was quite a change for him. He had just realised that he need no longer hide his feelings. He couldn't. The irony was not so much in the raw expression on his face but the uncertainty of what was to come.

Jack's mother had died two days earlier and he had not slept since. He kept on looking at his left wrist when he sensed that I was not looking at him. So, I asked him whether he had a prior engagement and if so, whether he wanted to finish the session early? Jack was looking at me intently as he burst into tears and began sobbing. Silence followed.

After composing himself, Jack reluctantly told me that he did not have a prior engagement. He looked like a man who had just been pulled out of a deep well, soaking wet. He said that he had placed his watch on his mother's wrist in the coffin before she was buried. Jack's final gesture was a powerful statement about his true feelings which he could no longer contain.

❋

There are forces operating in you to hold in check your basic primitive and self-serving impulses. It may be hard for you to deal with these forces which include guilt, which is a force too strong, too lasting, too destructive and often ineffective in the end. Envy and jealousy (the difference being that envy involves your wanting something that someone else has and jealousy involves your being afraid of losing something that you have), hatred, resentment, and all those other unwanted feelings.

Jealousy has been found to be transposable from early loss experiences or emotional withholding from opposite gender parents to adult interactions where the fear of abandonment by the beloved is often confused with jealousy. Fear of abandonment is not fear of loss. It is fear of rejection derived from a deep-rooted sense of inadequacy that may have nothing to do with the current status quo. The original loss experienced may have no sexual dimension but only a compulsive manifestation in adult life. So you ask, is jealousy real or imagined? It can be both.

It may be hard for you to carry these powerful feelings in your daily life. So why do you? It may be that feelings were not accepted in your early life and you were told to 'get your act together' when you expressed something emotional. You may have witnessed situations where feelings got out of control and you observed others experience extremes of feelings, which led you to decide never to be that way yourself. You may have been laughed at, made to feel inadequate or labelled as being 'weak' for showing your feelings. These may explain how you learned to bottle up your feelings, but they do not explain why you do it today.

As long as you continue to hold on to and bottle up your feelings it is safe. You do not have to expose yourself to any more risks and vulnerabilities. This becomes your way of preventing anyone from getting close to you. It is a constant reminder of what happens to you when you let others too near. Hence, you get caught between wanting closeness and feeling you are unable to achieve this without adverse consequences.

When you hide your feelings inside, you also prevent others from knowing how you feel. Although this may give you a sense of control; you are left to your own devices to fulfil your needs and consequently feel resentful that others don't care enough about you to reciprocate in kind. However, most of us bottle up our feelings because we feel that to express them is worse.

Jane's Story

Jane was having difficulty reconciling her life after seven years of marriage. She would often feel depressed, especially when she looked at herself closely and realised that she had bottled up her real self for such a long time.

Jane was a very intelligent woman who had graduated with honours from university. She met her husband whilst they were both training in an employer sponsored training program.

After completing their training, Jane and Tom, unable to express their attraction towards each other and not realising that they would eventually end up getting married, went their own way for several years.

Jane was attending a conference with her boyfriend in Singapore. During a break, she noticed Tom sitting around a table, talking to a few colleagues. Her immediate thought was to interrupt the discussion and ask Tom to join her for a drink. However, when she remembered that her boyfriend was waiting for her in their room, she decided against it.

A month later, Jane was asked by her employer to visit the company's Los Angeles office, to make sure that business was operating smoothly. Over several days of hard work, Jane managed to audit the business, delegate responsibility so the business would continue running smoothly, prepare a progress report for her employer back at home and make some time to catch up with friends.

On the weekend, Jane asked a few friends to join her for a drive down to San Diego, where she had planned to go sailing. Jane and her friends arrived at the San Diego marina and were organising a boat cruise for the day. Before they set sail, they decided to have lunch at the marina.

They had just settled at their table, when Jane saw Tom walking towards them. Tom had been in San Diego for two weeks on business and was also planning on doing some sailing. Jane asked Tom to join them. Tom was quick to accept the invitation and delighted to catch up with Jane.

When they returned from sailing, Jane and Tom decided to spend the rest of their weekend together. They also decided to fly back to Melbourne on the same flight.

Upon their return, Jane found that she could no longer continue her current relationship and was wanting to see more of Tom.

Tom was also having difficulty with his relationship and decided to confront his girlfriend knowing that his real reason for the confrontation was to end the relationship. After their weekend together, Tom was also wanting to see more of Jane.

Jane and Tom started to see each other regularly. After six weeks of courting, Jane accepted Tom's invitation to move in with him. A year later they got married and were happy with the progress they were both making. However, when they got married, the relationship started to shift.

Jane was working long hours and was frequently asked to travel overseas. Tom on the other hand, was beginning to feel frustrated with his work, envious of Jane's professional autonomy and angry that Jane was not making more time for him. During their courting, Jane and Tom decided that they would both work hard, save some money and buy their own house and have their own family.

However, they had not agreed on how this was to be achieved. The reality was that they were gradually becoming more distant from each other. The arguments over where they should live and how they should live their life together, were also becoming much more frequent. They were both stuck in a power struggle.

Jane was no longer wanting to travel for an hour in

the mornings to get to work. Although, this was a problem for Tom as well, he was reluctant to sell the house which they had bought from his brother.

Eventually, they started living separate lives. If Jane and Tom had continued taking care of themselves and each other the way they naturally did while they were courting, their relationship would have continued to grow.

However, the situation continued to deteriorate over the next several years. Jane found that she could no longer communicate with Tom, in the way she had during their courting days. They rarely ate together and they spent their weekends apart.

Jane liked going for walks by the beach and visiting bookshops and galleries. Tom was not interested in these activities. He would often jump into his convertible, get some friends together and go winery hunting, only to come home in a drunken state, ready for a fight.

Tom and Jane were waiting for something to happen to save their marriage. They both feared a confrontation and neither was willing to take responsibility to speak out about the sorry state of their marriage.

One day, out of frustration and realising that her marriage was heading for a breakdown, Jane called Tom and suggested that they should seek counselling together to see if they could salvage their marriage.

Tom would not have a bar of this. He maintained that she was the problem and, therefore, she should seek therapy, which Jane did. Therapy only cemented Jane's conviction that she wanted out of the marriage.

Late at work one night, Jane was invited to have a drink with a colleague, Brian. He was an articulate, ambitious and cultured man a decade older than Jane, and also having marital difficulties. After a couple of bottles of wine, he was no longer anxious about sharing his marital difficulties with Jane, who reciprocated in kind.

They understood each other. Jane and Brian rang their respective partners, just to make sure that they were where they were supposed to be and checked into a hotel nearby.

Tom was suspicious because Jane's call was quite unusual. She rarely called him from work. Tom decided to visit Jane at work. He parked his car in front of her office complex and saw that the light in Jane's office was turned off. In sheer suspicion and jealousy, he walked to the bar nearby looking for any signs of Jane.

After a few drinks, he got up to drive back home when he noticed Jane kissing Brian. At that moment, Tom felt great pain at what he saw and relief at what he felt. For months, he had been trying to tell Jane about his affair with his secretary.

After the bar incident, Jane and Tom sought counselling together. In the neutral counselling environment, they were both able to express their feelings towards each other. The heated sessions would often explode into vociferous arguments where they would blame the failure of the marriage on each other.

Neither Tom nor Jane were prepared to take responsibility for their failure. However, they did manage to work through their differences. Although the marriage ended, Tom and Jane agreed to disagree about their relationship issues and resolved to remain friends.

Understanding why you bottle up your feelings and beginning to unravel the different feelings affecting you at different times will not only be of great benefit to you, but it will also help you to prevent displacing your unwanted feelings on to others and thereby improve your relationships.

11
the road to assertiveness

What is assertiveness? How are people who are assertive in their interactions with others, different from other people? Why do we feel good about interacting with assertive people? Is assertiveness contagious?

Have you ever asked yourself any of these questions? Well, rather than looking at what assertiveness is not, here we will focus on what assertiveness is. Assertiveness is often confused with aggressiveness.

Assertiveness is NOT aggressiveness. Assertiveness is your ability to express yourself in an open, honest, consistent, forthright, firm, caring and considerate manner. Assertive people tend to have an appreciation of their self-worth and boundaries, acknowledge the need for self and collective preservation, strive to achieve mutually reciprocating, enriching and lasting relationships, accept responsibility for the consequences of their actions and are intrinsically motivated. Assertiveness is a skill that can be learned. Exposure to assertive role models in the formative years of life will no doubt make it easier.

When you are open and honest with other people, thoughtful of your own needs, but at the same time considerate and respecting of other people's, fair, firm, direct and equal in your relationships, you feel good about yourself. This reinforces increased motivation to accomplish your goals and brings people closer to you. It nurtures confidence, self-respect and a feeling of cooperation.

Other assertive people who interact with you respond to you with openness, honesty, cooperation and respect. Passive and aggressive people will initially respond to you with fear and antagonism but, with continued association, understand that you are not to be feared and disliked. With some people, this may be too much to expect.

When your motivation in being assertive is primarily to express yourself, including your thoughts, feelings, needs, and actions, to reach out to others, to stand up for what is yours, to express friendship, warmth and affection or sometimes anger, others will interpret and experience your confidence, friendship, honesty and reciprocate in kind.

When you behave assertively, by direct eye contact, by being firm rather than confrontational, by espousing positive and optimistic attitudes towards other people and life generally, by being unambiguous and emotionally generous, by not confusing your own legitimate rights and the rights of others, by being forthcoming rather than being secretive and withholding, other people will pay attention to you, acknowledge your rights and respect your needs.

Some may disagree and express anger towards you. However, within a friendly environment, constructive disagreements and the expression of anger is accepted rather than scorned. Remember your assertiveness will help others know where they stand, define boundaries and in return, assert themselves.

Assertiveness can be learned.

Alice's Story

Alice learned to be assertive the hard way. Although Alice is an extreme example of just how much some people have to suffer before they learn to stand up for themselves, once learned, it becomes easier for us to reach out to others.

My first impression of Alice was that she was a timid person who seemed emotionally uncomfortable and afraid. Her presence radiated a feeling that she was cramped for space, hungry for emotional freedom and yet anxious to explore herself. She seemed at times emotionally paralysed and was unable to maintain eye contact. I do not have the same effect on all my patients!

It took Alice a long time to open up. When she finally did, it was difficult to keep her on track. She was a polite and reserved twenty-four year old woman, born and raised in a remote village in eastern Turkey. She was only four years old when her father, mother, older sister and two brothers got on the plane and travelled across to the other side of the world and came to Australia.

Alice did not have many happy memories of her childhood. Her father often physically and emotionally abused her. She had vague memories of her father using violence as a form of discipline and control. When Alice was ten, her mother was hit by a passing car and went into a vegetable-like catatonic state. Alice took over the role of mother in the family.

Alice was taken out of school to cook, clean and look after her mother and her siblings. Her father had difficulty coping with his wife's predicament, became increasingly withdrawn and found solace in alcohol. He would often avoid coming home until late and when at home refused to partake in family activities. This chronic situation continued for five years when Alice's mother became pregnant. Alice was encapsulated in this closed world until her father decided it was time that she got married and to this end, took the family back to Turkey.

Alice felt immense relief when she arrived back in her village. She was no longer responsible for her family and the other relatives helped out in taking care of her parents.

Whilst her father was busy arranging a suitable husband for his daughter, she was making other plans for herself. Alice, partly to escape from her family and partly because she felt she needed someone to look after her, arranged to elope with a young man, who turned out to be a distant cousin. When she eventually returned home with her husband to be, her father severely assaulted her and she had to be taken to hospital for treatment.

A year later, with her father's consent, Alice married the young man she eloped with and returned to Australia. The rest of the family decided to remain in Turkey.

Once in Australia, Alice's husband began to abuse her physically and emotionally. She became pregnant and found it difficult to cope with the never ending accusations and threats.

Only when the physical and emotional pain became unbearable and her husband told her that he agreed to marry her to get out of the miserable village and come to Australia, did Alice pack up and leave. She spent the next year in a state of desperation. She moved into her parent's vacant house, gave birth and instituted legal proceedings to end the marriage.

Alice had difficulty resuming a family life with her parents, upon their return to Australia. They blamed her for the failure of her marriage and pressured her relentlessly to go back with her husband. When they realised that she was not going to reconcile with her husband, they changed tact and began pressuring her to marry again.

A year later, Alice's father arranged her second marriage. He convinced her to go along with this by arguing that her son needed a father. Alice liked the looks of her second husband.

That was the best .it was going to get. Although initially displaying a facade of a man who wanted to get married, have a family and children, problems emerged almost immediately. Her second husband had difficulty accepting the child from the first marriage and would often become violent towards the child and towards Alice, when she tried to protect him. He would often drive the child to her parent's house and leave him there.

Alice found herself in a helpless situation. She missed her child desperately. When she expressed her need to see and be with her child, she would be subjected to beatings.

The situation continued to deteriorate for another year. After her husband found out that Alice had broken her promise not to see her child, he severely assaulted her. During the fight, he accused her of having affairs behind his back.

Alice decided at that point that she was no longer going to expose herself to more of the same punishment. She left her husband and filed assault charges against him with the police.

She has not seen her husband for over two years and has distanced herself from her parents. Her older sister moved in with her parents after her divorce from her husband and although the father tried to coerce them both into marrying again, they have not taken him seriously.

Alice, like most non-assertive people, found it difficult to express herself. The dilemma is that by not owning up to what is yours and standing up for your rights in an assertive manner, you give other people the message that it is acceptable for them to treat you as they do. In a sense, you give others permission to take advantage of you. This is not healthy and eventually leads to great distress, hurt, pain and loss.

12
the road to
success

If you feel that success is something that everyone else has managed to achieve but not you, it is important that you keep this in perspective. People who do not see themselves as successful, often seem to arrange to avoid pleasure or success in a number of ways. They don't define clear benchmarks for their success, they hang on to their failures and diminish the importance of their achievements, and they perpetuate their failures by not learning from their mistakes.

Taken to the extreme, failure becomes an unconscious device to punish those around you for what you perceive to be their contribution to your hopeless predicament.

You may have achieved high marks in a subject and proceeded to mess up the next exam paper, arranged an important meeting for a career move and missed the appointment, started a serious relationship and continued casual affairs in secret.

You may genuinely want to succeed, but you sabotage your success by not allowing yourself to fully achieve it. Most of the time, you sabotage your success because your feeling of success has become closely linked with guilt, self blame or with something perceived as being unobtainable. This association is not a conscious thought, but a powerful undermining process.

The resolution requires that you relearn certain things. If you have incorporated into your being the idea that you really aren't entitled to very much, it is quite difficult to start to claim ownership to what is rightfully yours. You are not responsible for the depressed, miserable, and unhappy lives of those around you.

You have the right to make the best of your life without having to apologise or feel guilty about it. Remember the Golden Rule is: *Do unto others as you would have others do unto you.* Not: *Let others do unto you what ever they would like to do.*

Confronting just how much you have sabotaged your success can be a depressing task, especially if there is a lot of it. Taking stock of your losses and putting them into perspective may relieve some of your confusion and give you a basis to start again.

It is important to remember that once you have learned to consolidate what is inside you by accepting what belongs to you and attributing appropriate responsibility for what belongs to others, you will be in a better position to stand up to those who have reinforced your self negation. You need to consistently stand up for who you are and resist those who have encouraged you to be otherwise.

Alex's Story

Alex paid a costly price for not standing up for himself. He was a single man in his thirties, brought up in a professional home with an older brother and two younger sisters. Several years before he came to therapy, Alex had an emotional breakdown which left him stunted. This situation culminated in him first being admitted to a local psychiatric hospital for several weeks and upon discharge, referral to long-term therapy.

Alex manifested an intractable form of self sabotage which was marked by depressive and mild paranoid features and which appeared in two different types of circumstance. One was when he was frustrated by other people, when in his rage he would feel like destroying everything good of his own. The other was when he was offered satisfaction for his needs, he would feel like destroying the thing he was being offered and attacking the person who offered it to him.

Alex spent his childhood and adolescence in private boarding schools. He was a poor student and was frequently before the academic disciplinary board. He often got into fights and was eventually expelled.

His parents were both high achievers, well respected in their professions and imposed great expectations on their children. At the age of thirteen, his father took Alex to a psychiatrist. Alex remembers sitting in the cold room with his father pointing his index finger at him, whilst focusing his eyes directly at the doctor and saying: *fix him*. To this day, Alex is still at a loss to understand why he was taken to the doctor. His apathy towards his parents prevented him from asking them. His parent's enrolled him at another boarding school, even further away from home.

He was soon after branded as the *black sheep* in the family. Unable to match the academic and sporting achievements of his older brother and sisters, Alex began feeling a deep hatred towards his family. Alex refused to study. At one stage he even refused to go to school and was recommended to be taken out.

At sixteen, Alex ran away from home and had no contact with his family for another two years. One night he was picked up by the police, half unconscious slumped under a bridge. After a week in hospital, his father was contacted and asked to come and take him home. Although the family's initial response was one of concern, their good for nothing attitude towards Alex soon began to surface.

Alex felt that he could not communicate with his parents and was too envious and resentful of his siblings to talk to them. His older brother had left the family home and was completing his medical internship at a country hospital. One of his sisters had married and moved out and the other was at university.

There was no room for Alex. He became the boiling point of many family feuds. As a last resort, his mother purchased an apartment for him, furnished it and helped Alex start his own life. However, Alex felt as though he had been imprisoned and conveniently taken care of by his parents.

Spending long hours by himself, Alex found it difficult to establish friendships. He felt inadequate with men and feared rejection by women. He thought about selling his mother's apartment and using the proceeds to travel abroad, but decided against it when he realised that he would have to go back to living with his parents when he returned.

Alex was stuck. He blamed his parents for his hopeless predicament. He often found solace in the thought that once his parents were gone (which from his point of view was not too far away!) he would inherit his share of their wealth and that would make up for his loss. At this thought he would feel deep guilt, self hatred and anger fused together and proceeded to decide on a way of killing himself. He would then feel sorry for himself, angry at his parents and the whole cycle would continue as it had for so long.

Alex often felt that life had little to offer him. He could not see anything positive in himself or his family. He felt powerless and inadequate. He had lived his life proving to himself and others that he was a failure. Not his, but his parent's failure. He had no idea where to begin to break this cycle.

Both his inner depressive feelings of emptiness and guilt and the outside paranoid feelings of persecution were relieved when Alex was able to acknowledge their origin in the destructive feelings within himself. These feelings in turn owed their origin to his sense of deprivation, which was directed towards his parents and more specifically towards those people who had given to him in the past and those who gave to him now.

The solution, quite ironically, was in himself. No one could make up for what Alex had missed out on. He had to work through his anger about what he felt he was deprived of, his self-destructive tendencies and his self-worth issues. Through his long and often challenging recovery, Alex learned to take responsibility for his own life, stop sabotaging himself and stop failing in life to satisfy his feeling of being disappointed.

13

the road to oedipus and electra

There was a prophecy made by the Oracle at Delphi that King Liaus and Queen Jocasta of Thebes were going to have a son who was fated to kill the father. Imagine if the Oracle at Delphi had prophesised that King Liaus and Queen Jocasta of Thebes were going to have a daughter who was fated to kill the mother. She would have killed her mother, married her father and in a wild rage blinded herself.

Just imagine if the Oracle at Delphi had prophesised that King Liaus and Queen Jocasta of Thebes were going to have a daughter who was fated to kill her father. She would have killed her father, married her mother and in total confusion blinded herself. Or what if the poor Oracle at Delphi was just wrong? As it turns out, the prophecy did unfold. A son Oedipus was born, and the fatalistic King and

Queen ordered a servant to take the boy and leave him naked by a mountainside.

However, Oedipus was saved and brought up at Corinth. When he had grown up, Oedipus met a chariot on the road. He was provoked into a fight and killed both charioteer and his passenger, without knowing that the passenger he had just killed was his father, King Laius. The murderer's identity remained unknown.

Moving on to Thebes, Oedipus solved the riddle of the Sphinx and was granted the hand of the recently widowed Queen Jocasta. When Oedipus later discovered that he had killed his father, King Liaus and married his mother Queen Jocasta, out of intense remorse and self-punishment he blinded himself.

On the face of it there seems nothing unique about this story. Ancient Greek mythology is full of similar tragedies concerned with the murder of relatives of one kind or another, and sexual impulses towards kins. However, although no one speaks of the 'Electra complex' to refer to a daughter's murderous feelings towards her mother, the Oedipus myth has survived history like a fossil and through the genius of Freud, planted itself in psychology as the 'Oedipus Complex'.

Sorting through oedipal feelings is like walking through a minefield. The far reaching implications extend to family dynamics in two ways. Firstly, when the parents are alive but are perceived as being noticeably weak or overwhelmingly strong figures and secondly when one parent has abandoned ship or died at a crucial stage in the child's development. Whether there is parental loss or not, the effects can be quite powerful and at times debilitating.

If there is no parental loss, inherent problems may still emerge. For example, if the parent of the same sex is seen as a rival for the parent of the opposite sex, then intense competitive feelings and deep seated hostility on the one hand and intense guilt and fear of retribution on the other, would be a natural consequence.

The death or absence of a parent, whether by design or accident can have far reaching consequences for us, especially if the loss occurred during our formative years. The subsequent oedipal feelings that develop may give rise to various symptoms that to us may seem to come from nowhere.

The universal clue is that because we have missed out on fathering or mothering, we are likely to seek these in other people who come to represent our parents. Taken to the extreme, for example, you may find that you are frequently ill and therefore have to often go to the doctor, who's profession is caring for people.

Harry's Story

Harry was referred as an emergency patient by his doctor who felt that Harry should be assessed and taken on for long-term therapy as soon as practicable. The urgency in the doctor's voice and the fact that he had called me himself indicated that the matter was serious.

There was a vacancy following a cancellation that afternoon and Harry was on his way. In discussing Harry's medical history with the doctor prior to the appointment, it became clear that Harry was not your usual patient. His father died when Harry was fourteen whilst he was still in Syria.

Harry was brought up by his older brother and mother and was quite happy with his life until he was called to do his military service just prior to the war with Israel.

Harry's brother who worked as a diplomat and had contacts within the government bureaucracy arranged for Harry to escape military service. The plan was that he would go with his mother to New Zealand and his brother would follow them once they were settled.

After a brief stay in New Zealand and finding it difficult to find employment, Harry persuaded his mother to settle in Sydney. Harry and his mother both managed to find jobs straight away.

After sharing a small flat with another family for a few weeks, they managed to secure a large house close to the beach. They were both eagerly waiting for Harry's older brother who had taken over responsibility both as surrogate husband and father, to arrive.

However, Harry's brother had decided to stay in Syria and get married. Whilst Harry felt abandoned and let down by his brother, his problems didn't start for another two years.

He came home from work one evening to find an ambulance outside his house. They were taking his mother out of the house on a stretcher. She had collapsed after a major stroke and was on her way to the local hospital.

Harry was never to see his mother alive again. He returned to an empty home and sat outside on the front porch for several hours staring into oblivion.

Harry subsequently asked his employer for a transfer to Melbourne. He had an uncle in Melbourne and felt happy at the thought of being with his uncle. After several months in Melbourne, Harry's job was made redundant.

With what little money he had saved up and with the support of his uncle, he opened up a coffee shop. Harry knew very little about running a small business and soon found himself in debt. Harry was an optimist. He didn't mind the hard work but he was not prepared for the demands of running a business. He often felt strained that things were getting out of control and he reacted with equal impulsiveness. Harry took matters in his own hands and sacked all the staff. He found himself working from six in the morning to late at night. After eight months of hard work, he managed to turn the business around and sell it. He was beginning to feel free again.

Late one night on his way home, Harry felt that the other passengers on the train were staring at him. He felt as if the world was closing in on him. He felt anxious. His heart was pounding. He felt fear. He had to get away. Although his house was another three stops away, he got off at the next station. He walked the rest of the way home and found it difficult to get to sleep. His anticipation was overwhelming. In the morning he went to see his doctor who gave him a script and asked him to come back in a couple of days if he was still feeling the same.

When Harry arrived back at his house, the phone was ringing. It was his brother calling him to let him know that he was planning a business trip to Hong Kong and that he would be coming to visit Harry at the end of the month.

Harry had not seen his brother since he left Syria. He did not know how he felt about the news. His brother had made similar promises of visiting Harry in the past, but had always cancelled at the last moment. He felt guilt at the thought of telling his brother to go to hell, and managed to put the phone down without unleashing his anger. After all, he had taken care of Harry, hadn't he?

After Harry put the phone down, he remembered the death of his father, the move to New Zealand with his mother and feeling let down by his brother, the death of his mother in Sydney and the loss of his job and small business, the isolation, the failure and the anger. But he still loved his brother.

Harry started attending doctors frequently. From the time of the phone call from his brother to the due date of his brother's arrival, he had visited all the doctors and hospitals in his area as well as arranging home visits over the phone.

A survey of the professionals involved in Harry's treatment revealed that he had sought treatment for more than a dozen different ailments. His presentation was also consistent.

He would rush in to the Centre and demand to be

examined immediately with vociferous displays of impending death. Finding very little physically wrong with him, the doctors would either prescribe him some medication or refer him on in frustration. After a while, Harry would begin feeling that his complaints were not taken seriously and not turn up to his appointments. In frustration and contempt at not getting what he really needed, Harry would move on to another doctor who was not familiar with him. Harry's cycle had thus continued for some time.

Except this time he was coming to see me. I greeted Harry downstairs and he followed me to the consulting room. He was a big man with grey roots showing in his brown hair. Once in the room he waited for me to sit down and began pacing.

He did not know where to start. After describing his fragmented life, he sat down. We were to see each other for another two years. I am happy to report that Harry has finally come to terms with his parental loss and has decided to visit his brother who now lives in London.

I could not pretend for a moment to be able to give to him what his family couldn't. Harry was able to accept what he had been deprived of and work through his anger about having missed out on fathering and to a lesser extent, mothering.

Therapy only served to help Harry become aware of the dynamics of his behaviour and to understand why he needed to repeat these dynamics with everybody with whom he interacted. Harry did the rest himself.

Sometimes early loss of a parent which is not mourned properly produces guilt in the child. This may surface unconsciously and sabotage the child's later life. If you lost a parent during your childhood, you may have felt guilt about the death, especially if you favoured the living parent and therefore like Oedipus, felt disturbed about gaining something from it. You may have disguised your guilt by idealisation of the dead parent. If you have lost a parent how has this been for you?

Men who have lost a father during their childhood, do sometimes have difficulty relating to other men. This is more so if there were no other adequate role models after the father's death. The difficulty is often in the form of hostility towards male authority figures.

Encouraged by the widowed mother who leans towards her son as a replacement husband, some men feel that they have to over-compensate for not having had a father by being more in control, strong, powerful and successful to make up for the loss. This often leads to more problems for a young boy who grows up way before his time, trying to fit into a dead man's shoes. Stunted, the 'fatherless child' is left behind lonely, sad, cut off and unable to claim his manliness.

A man who loses his mother during his childhood may be deprived of maternal nurturing and feminine influence, thus creating difficulties in his relationships with women. He may deny his need for mothering or over-compensate for the lack of mothering by becoming mothering towards others himself.

Women who have lost their father during childhood often grow up having difficulty relating to men in fear of losing them. The young girl may feel insecure in her femininity as regards to men and idealise the dead father whatever he was like. She may find it difficult to find a man for herself who matches the perfect man that her father has become and because she has been so disappointed herself, she may want to disappoint other people without realising why.

Losing a mother, especially for a child is a frightening experience. The feeling of loss may continue throughout the child's development.

From the time of the mother's death, the emotional, instinctual and intuitional aspects of the young girl may be stunted as she struggles to survive without a mother. In her later life, she may seek mothering from others or quickly become a mother herself or avoid mothering altogether as a way of dealing with the painful feeling of loss.

What about those children who have never had the opportunity of knowing their father and in some cases mother?

Clinical evidence suggests that in such people one frequently finds the same feelings, usually incorporating a fantasy of an authoritarian parent who is ruthless, strict and disapproving of the person's sexuality in any form, towards whom the person feels a mixture of fear and hostility.

In situations where parental loss occurs at a young age, the person's whole inner world may become dominated by the loss, thereby preventing their full development into mature adults.

What of those children who have grown up living with the consequences of parental separation? Children suffer the most when a marriage or a partnership breaks down.

Parents are the child's anchor to the physical and emotional world and to have this threatened can have devastating consequences. The separating parents need to understand that their anger and hatred for each other can never be as important or more than their love for their children.

The impact of the separation can be alleviated by the way in which parents behave after the separation. By not forcing their children to take sides and helping the children understand that they are not to blame for the parent's separation can lessen the effects of the trauma.

Parents with a young child who are working towards separation need to remember that the young child may have no memory of the actual separation but they will absorb and retain inside the atmosphere and feelings of those undergoing the separation.

Parents may attempt to rationalise their behaviour to deal with feelings of anger, guilt, self blame, fear and the like by maintaining that what they are doing is in the child's best interests. Parents may go so far as to say to their child: It's your father I'm leaving not you. However, the feeling of not being good enough or of rejection is no less devastating.

A girl whose father leaves the family during her transition phase from childhood to adolescence has to contend not only with losing a father but also having to deal with her feelings of rejection as a growing woman. A girl who feels rejected by her father may develop a hatred and envy of everything masculine, and a compulsive need to compete with men.

Underneath these feelings there often lies a deep sense of inferiority to men and other women and a corresponding depreciation of everything feminine. It would not be an unrealistic consequence to expect such women to want to dominate their own sex and punish the opposite sex.

A son whose father leaves the family during his transition phase from childhood to adolescence, may find it difficult to cope with his new role of surrogate husband with his mother whilst at the same time missing and wanting to be with his father.

When a mother leaves the family and children, the impact is just as great. The children may feel a sense of not being good enough for her to stay or that somehow they are to blame for the mother's behaviour. The feeling of rejection is also strong.

14

the road to a productive partnership

The original title for this chapter was *The Road to a Successful Relationship*. However, these days relationships have taken on their own identities quite separate from the people involved. Each historical era has developed its own understanding of what constitutes a relationship. In contemporary modern society relationships are just as important as ever. Unfortunately, relationships have become dispensable, just like almost everything else today. Therefore, a more appropriate framework focusing on the interaction between individuals seems necessary.

This is one context where the sums of the parts are equal to, if not greater than the whole. It implies that outside of a relationship, the individual is just as important and worthy as they are in a relationship. A relationship can only develop and mature if two people want this to happen. It takes only one person to dissolve a relationship and two to make it work. Outside of a relationship, each individual is capable of existing in the full richness of life.

The problems begin when two people unaware of each other's intellectual compatibility, common interests and ideals and are shellshocked by what they call love, decide to get together. The analogy of a football team and a soccer team, with their respective rules, attempting to play a game against each other, would suffice to highlight the potential problems awaiting a couple at this stage in the relationship. The nature of their differences would compel each person to strive to exert their preferred rules, thereby establishing the foundations of a relationship based on competition rather than mutual support.

It may not always be obvious but, most people who decide to become emotionally involved, do so because they want to be happy. So, what happens to these people who get together? At the outset everything is exciting. They exchange feelings, thoughts and ideals. They spend a lot of time together, often doing no more than just enjoying each other's company. There are no hidden agendas, resentments or suspicions. Then something happens and both are at a loss as to what went wrong. Earlier unrealistic illusions become replaced with hard reality.

This is the point at which most people get stuck. If separation follows, the extent of their emotional pain and anguish will be equivalent to the extent of their emotional investment and the degree of significance attached to the relationship or person.

Although you may have heard the saying *time heals all wounds*, this sort of emotional pain is not time contingent. The solution is to re-evaluate your emotional investment and look at why you have made this person so significant in your life.

It is only natural that if two people decide to get together, some time will be spent testing each other and defining what is acceptable and what is not. If you are able to reach a realistic compromise, then stability will follow.

If you are unable to achieve a realistic compromise, you need to think carefully about where you want to go from here. If you have not been able to achieve a sense of balance in your life and pretend that everything is well, then you are likely to join a large number of people who have cornered the divorcee market.

The basic premise underlying a productive partnership is cooperation rather than competition. Within this atmosphere people are able to share, express and experience genuine feelings such as trust, caring, affection, warmth and growth.

Even anger, expressed in a constructive fashion, has its place.

Regardless of other achievements, such as wealth, power, status and the like, any person who has not experienced a true friendship, predicated upon the fundamental notion of cooperation and reciprocation rather than superficiality and competition, is emotionally deprived and disadvantaged.

15
the point of no return

You have covered a vast amount of distance in your journey so far. To appreciate just how far you have travelled, imagine that you are standing at a beach facing the ocean. Ahead of you is a fifty-metre wave. It is coming towards you. Now, for most people the thought of confronting such a wave conjures up images of being carried off and tossed around, and ending up being injured or slumped unconscious in some remote place. Other people imagine that they can stop or resist the wave. At this stage of your journey, your only real choice is to let the wave carry you, because it is going in the same direction as you are heading.

Have you ever noticed that when you have travelled to a particular destination for the first time, it has taken you longer to reach your destination than to return? What was your destination? At the point of no return, you have reached a point where you cannot go back. You cannot close your eyes and remain oblivious to your thoughts, feelings and actions. At this point, if you were to attempt to regress, it will take you longer to return to the beginning, than it will take you to continue to the end.

I think it was Galileo who said that if you stand in the same spot you are standing on and continue walking, you would eventually reach the same spot you started from. In life, by virtue of experience and learning, once we reach the point of no return, we can't just simply go back to the starting point.

Cybil's Story

Cybil started walking along the path of a long distance relationship at the age of twenty-one.

Cybil was an only child and received all the love and attention that two loving, caring and protective parents could provide. During her final year of university, she went interstate to be the Maid of Honour at her best friend's wedding. Here, she met Sam, the best man of the groom. Cybil and Sam had never met before and they spent the night dancing away. Towards the end of the wedding Sam invited the bridal party to his place.

Cybil was at a crossroad, to go or not to go? She decided to join the bridal party and had Sam's undivided attention throughout the whole evening. Sam offered to take her back to the hotel she was staying at. Cybil accepted the offer and like a true gentleman, Sam drove her to her hotel. They exchanged phone numbers and parted ways.

Sam called Cybil early in the morning and wished her a safe flight back home. He promised to keep in touch, and he did. As time went on Cybil and Sam started seeing more of one another, commuting to and from each State. By this stage Cybil had come across many crossroads, and little did she know that there were many more to follow. She got to know Sam and his family more closely. She noticed a strong bond between Sam and his mother.

Sam was a young, carefree accountant who worked in a medium sized accounting firm. Prior to meeting Cybil, Sam spent a lot of his spare time with his family. Cybil felt that Sam's mother started to resent her because he was now spending his spare time with her.

Cybil's parents also started voicing some major concerns about this man she had been spending a lot of time with. They were seeing less of Cybil and weren't that convinced that Sam was the right man for her.

After almost two years of commuting between States, Cybil and Sam decided to get married. However, they faced another crossroad, one of them would have to relocate. They spent a considerable amount of time discussing the possibilities. Upon completing her degree, Cybil started working in a clerical job. Sam on the other hand, had been with the accounting firm for three years. It made sense to both of them that Cybil move to be with Sam.

Upon breaking the news to her parents, Cybil came straight out with the plans she had discussed with Sam. She told them that they planned to marry and that she would be moving interstate. Her parents were disappointed. They felt their daughter could do better for herself. But Cybil felt that even if she chose to marry a prince they would still put up a fight. She tried to reassure them that she would be happy and they should be happy for her.

So they started planning. Cybil spent a lot of time planning the wedding while Sam was happy to go along with the decisions she made. Sam's family tried to get involved in the planning but Cybil felt that to avoid conflict, it was best that they stay out of it. After many months of trying to organise a wedding interstate, Cybil was getting quite frustrated with the lack of support from Sam. She felt she couldn't ask her parents for support because she was making a life decision against their will. She felt Sam had no interest in the wedding plans. He even started spending less time with her.

This went on for a couple of months. Two weeks prior to the wedding, when Cybil was at the dressmakers for the bridesmaid's dress fitting, she received a phone call from Sam. Out of the blue, Sam started objecting to Cybil's bridal party. He suggested that one of his cousins be a bridesmaid.

This really struck a cord in Cybil. With only two weeks to go to the wedding Sam decided to make a contribution to the planning.

It's a bit late don't you think, said Cybil. She knew that it wasn't Sam talking to her but his mother who wanted to intervene in her choice of bridesmaids and groomsmen. It was at that point that Cybil started to realise that she wasn't just marrying Sam, but she was also marrying his mother. Cybil's response to Sam at that moment's was: *tell your mother, the wedding is off.*

Cybil saw a glimpse of her life with Sam. As the union got closer, Sam's mother became more controlling and intrusive. She was frightened at the thought of being married to her mother-in-law. She wanted a partner. Not a child. At that crossroad, she had thought about the three years she had invested into this relationship. She realised that for Sam, she was a prize; like a car he deserved, to make his sacrifice for his family worthwhile. A trophy to make him feel better. Cybil realised that she wanted a life partner and felt that the best option would be to continue moving forward. She put it down to *cold feet*.

Cybil did not feel like she was back at the starting point. She didn't look back and regret the decision she made at her point of no return. Imagine living with someone who is so spoilt that they refuse to grow up and whose mother is competing with you for the rest of your life?

16
the road to reality

We are a strange lot. We sometimes plan things knowing that they will not work out. In most instances, however, things don't always turn out the way they were planned. Our judgement is not always accurate. Our needs are powerful and operate in complex ways. The reality is that we are the unsuspecting victims of our own personalities. This is not a law. It is merely a factual observation about how things are.

Have you ever thought about those intangible and mysterious forces that gel the different aspects of our lives together?

Well, I have and there are many. Time, reason, faith, history, sanity, God, commitment, wisdom passion, reality, irony, responsibility, work, knowledge, imagination, love, certainty, inspiration and conscience, to name a few. How many more can you think of? In this chapter an attempt will be made to focus on one of these. Reality.

I was once running a group therapy program and I wanted to test whether the reality for me was the same reality for each of the participants in the group. However, first I had to make sure that there was enough rapport and cohesion between the group members. At the end of the fourth session, I felt that it was time.

After the fifth session began, I settled into my chair, sat for two minutes and just smiled. Later when I asked each participant to explain how they perceived my action, fourteen people interpreted this one reality in fourteen different ways. One thought that I had won the lottery. Another thought that I had a pleasant morning. Some thought that I had a pleasant evening the night before. So what is the reality?

Let me demonstrate what reality is. I do not know about you but I like coffee. I like my coffee with condensed milk and honey. How do you like yours? The reality is that there is only one coffee. Just because the coffee jars are shaped or labelled differently and come in a variety of colours and tastes, it does not mean that what is contained in each jar is not coffee; albeit different types of coffee.

So, it is not that there were fourteen different realities for the group participants, but fourteen different interpretations of the same reality. The context and meaning of reality therefore, can be found in the frame of reference used by people who define that particular reality.

To demonstrate this point, let me tell you about Allen.

Allen's Story

Allen was a bright young man who had difficulty with women. His difficulty was not so much in his interactions with women but in his inability to hold back. When Allen entered a relationship, he was genuinely loving and selflessly interested in his partner's well being. He would nurture his partner's growth and give unconditionally.

After a stormy two-year relationship that finally ended, he decided that he was going to be on his own for a while. However, he soon found himself attracted to an older woman. After six months of knowing each other and enjoying a rich and complex friendship, Allen moved in with Kate.

Kate had been married before and was reaching an age where she was eager to have a child and very adamant to get married. Allen on the other hand, was not so eager to have a child but had not discounted the possibility of getting married.

During the four months they lived together, Kate was overwhelmed with Allen's giving nature. She had not met anyone like Allen before and saw him as the solution to her problems. Her spiritual guru had enlightened her about what was going to make her life complete: *she needed a business, a husband and a child*. Kate was a doctor and together they were working towards establishing a medical centre. Allen had a child from a previous marriage and during access visits, he would often include Kate. Kate felt that Allen was a wonderful father and partner. Kate would often describe Allen to her friends as the man she had been waiting for, all her life.

However, Allen was conscious that he did not want to be incidental in Kate's life. After all, Kate could have a child with and marry anybody.

When Allen revealed his interpretation of reality to Kate, he was no longer the loving, caring and giving man. Kate began to feel that in order for her to be with Allen, she had to put her plans aside and conform to his expectations of her. Live her life according to his rules. Overnight, Allen became public enemy number one. Kate began telling her friends that Allen was just using her, that he was dangerous and that he did not deserve to exist.

What motivated Allen to seek a relationship with Kate had not altered. So, what happened? More specifically, what happened to Kate's interpretation of reality? It was no longer consistent with what was motivating her.

So, she just distorted reality a little to cope with the dissonance and the inevitable loss. This was nothing new for Kate. It was, as she often described during her therapy: *The story of her life.* Kate was predisposed to recreating her past reality. Allen merely fitted in. He was in fact incidental to Kate's life.

Reality is the fine line between what is and what is possible. If we cannot digest what is, then we may become a victim of what is possible. For example, a woman who refuses to accept that her husband is cheating on her, in spite of ample evidence to raise her suspicions, is not facing reality. What she is doing is trying to avoid reality. Facing reality may mean that she would have to consider ending her marriage. An unbearable and daunting proposition.

Reality is unique. It is unique in the sense that we all interpret reality according to the motivation behind our actions. However, sometimes reality is not palatable; sometimes it is painful and cruel.

17

the road to love

What about Love? There is not a word that is more disturbing, confusing, ambiguous, emotionally laden and powerful in any language.

People use love to express almost any feeling. They use it to denote feelings ranging from their secret and passionate desires to their basic likes. Sometimes they use love as a basis to justify their abuse, possessiveness and violence, at other times, they use it to let go. Some experience loss of love and grieve whilst others are enriched.

I would love to be able to tell you that I have discovered a formula for love, hitherto unknown. The fact is I haven't. The best I can do is offer you a simple explanation. According to this explanation, the amount of love you project to an outside object, which is what you claim to feel, can only be measured in extremes. That is, the amount you have invested in loving the object and your fear of the loss of the loved object can proportionally determine the meaning and value of the love you feel. Here, an assumption is made that your experience of love is experienced as an absolute. That is, you either love the object or you don't.

Why is it that love can sometimes blossom between two people and sometimes drain them? Chances are that if you were in a blossoming intimate friendship you may not have chosen to read this book. Therefore, let's look at how love can end up draining the beloved and the lover.

In this context love has many possible dimensions: physical, spiritual, emotional, romantic, sexual, sensual and more. I would like to offer one patient's experience of the richness and destructiveness of love in a relationship. This person whom we can call Mr. Fixit has evolved to be a subgroup of the collective representation of man in contemporary western culture.

Mr. Fixit is, basically, honest, doesn't mind and in fact looks forward to hard work, is caring, loving and unconditionally and unequivocally reciprocating towards his partner. No one asked him to be like this. Due to his own intrinsic drives, goals and personality, his natural inclination is to give to those whom he loves. There is nothing wrong with this. Here, I do not use the term "wrong" to imply a moral imperative.

What I mean is that Mr. Fixit is inherently conditioned to give to those whom he loves. This is fundamentally, to subconsciously introduce a reciprocal dimension to the relationship in order to establish loving, caring, nurturing interpersonal dynamics for a mutually rewarding and supportive sense of self-preservation. Afterall, aren't two hearts better than one? Maybe.

Somewhere along the line, Mr. Fixit begins to feel anger and resentment that his natural inclination is being taken advantage of or abused. The difficulty for Mr. Fixit is that he now also begins to feel frustrated because he does not know how, after having set so many precedents of encouraging his partner's dependence on him, to say: *No, I can't fix it.*

In reality, in attempting to care for and love those around him, Mr. Fixit has started to feel resentful because his own needs are being ignored. He cannot accept help and support from his partner because that is not the nature of his personality and, consequently, their relationship. He cannot take time out for himself because he feels guilty that he is not and should be with his partner.

As Mr. Fixit begins to experience awareness of his emotional deficiency he starts to become distant and resentful towards the ones he loves. At this point, he needs to take stock of his emotions and clarify his reasons for loving his partner and his reasons for being resentful and distant.

Mr. Fixit still loves his partner. It's just that he is becoming concerned at the personal cost of lack of unequivocal reciprocation from his partner that is at the core of his resentment.

It is possible for Mr. Fixit to love and resent his partner at the same time. It is even possible for Mr. Fixit to love and hate his partner at the same time. What he does with the love and hate is the real test of his character. So far, the evidence is that Mr. Fixit's contributes to the problems from the beginning. His attitude towards his partner and possibly the rest of the world is: *If there is a problem, tell me about it and we'll see if I can fix it*. The fact is that Mr. Fixit is not unequivocally reciprocating. He ought to be able to allow his partner to help out, be supportive and join in with the fixing. With the best of noble intentions, this is how Mr. Fixit sews the seeds of trouble in his relationships.

The fact is that Mr. Fixit is really a slave to his own insecurities. He not only does not know how to say no without feeling inadequate, but he also does not know what do with himself. So he fixes. If it is not broken, then he will break it only to compulsively to try to fix again and again. This what is I mean by a cycle.

What about Ms. I NEED A MAN TO FIXIT? She's not like this from the outset. She's honest, strong willed, hard working, innocent and most likely troubled by the issues in her life which require her to make decisions about whether she should live her life the way she wants or whether she should please others at her own personal cost.

Ms. I NEED A MAN TO FIXIT? isn't really ready to enter into an adult relationship. She is too ready to abandon her own drives, goals and future and adopt those of her partner. She needs to learn to compromise realistically.

If she can fix it herself, she shouldn't have to rely on Mr. Fixit to come to her rescue and when he starts taking over, she has a duty to herself to maintain her own boundaries and competencies, not compromise by her submissiveness and inclination to keep the peace and then resent him for it.

Like reality, there is also only one Love. The ingredients of love, when combined together, are so powerful, so demanding, so overwhelming and so enriching, that when exposed to it, we are left feeling vulnerable, yet absolute and certain. Love involves acceptance, responsibility, caring, empathy, consciousness and respect.

Like reality, love also comes in different shapes and sizes. Kings have thrown away their kingdoms for love. Men and women have refused to live without love. Others, with little success, have refused to die because of love.

Love is a passionate commitment to anything – music, reading, work, mankind, even life itself. You labour for that which you love and you love that for which you labour. The problem with this particular approach to love is that if you have not experienced love, you will have difficulty in showing it to others.

Don't you believe it! It is not that we have not experienced love, but that we have lost touch with the fact that we have all been loved. We just have difficulty recognising it.

Whether we like it or not, we were all born. Our mother whose love by the way is the epitome of all worldly love; laboured for us. She carried us in her womb until we saw light. After we were born, she did what ever she could, given her capacity and limitations, to make sure that we were nurtured. Her love was not conditional. We did not have to do anything in order to be loved; it was given to us unconditionally.

What of romantic love? This is epitomised in the

lyrics of a popular song: *'it must have been love, but it's over now, it must have been good, but I lost it somehow.'* This form of love is predicated on the notion that you are either attracted to someone who becomes the object of your love or that you seek out, consciously or unconsciously, certain people and project your love, only to end up losing them.

Our sexual and reproductive urges, our inability to cope with loneliness and our inherent drive to be with other people makes it easy for us to seek comfort in others. Love in this sense can be seen as an opportunistic attempt to fulfil our basic needs and therefore, is as quickly lost as it is gained. This is not love. It is a form of self-indulgence and entertainment. If you lack a basic understanding of the other person, are unable to see the person for who he or she is and accept them for who they are, you will find yourself feeling love which is destined to deteriorate into possessiveness, jealousy, conflict and eventually loss.

To love another person, you have to be able to relate to that person's existence. It is not about fear or loss. This form of love is not accidental. Nor is it haphazard. It is divorced from selfishness. It is about loving the other person as they are. Not as you would like them to be.

18

the road to irony

Why do we hurt the ones we love the most? This question is simple yet fundamentally profound and ironical. You would expect the opposite to be true. However, once again human irrationality prevails, even in this domain.

To understand this question we need to understand several key concepts. These concepts are not obvious at first. The reason why they are not obvious is that our reasoning cannot pinpoint the substance of these concepts without a framework. So, you might say, what is this framework?

If you have been able to follow so far we are on the right track. You see, I have taken you on a very short journey into what is called reasoning.

This ability that we are born with is a significant survival tool. It enables us to think, make inferences, predict behaviour and intentions, induce motivation and most important of all communicate. This is where the framework begins.

Communication is one of the essential ingredients in any relationship. In an emotional relationship, two people choose to explore the depths of each other's emotional existence.

The fluency and harmony in the other domains of the relationship is no guarantee of such, in the emotional world. Here the rules are different. It is because they are different that a lot of people walk around on this planet in a confused mental and emotional existence.

Let's go back to the original question, now that we understand the framework. Why do we hurt the ones we love the most? Hurt (a feeling experienced by someone who is on the receiving end of deprivation, punishment, sadistic intentions and actions, or through various other reasons, and a feeling that is difficult to experience unless one becomes the object of another's intention to hurt) is transient. It can be intractable but you have to want that.

This is where another human frailty lies. Within a loving atmosphere, we cause hurt to the ones who become the objects of our most intense feelings. Why should this be so?

When we stop loving or withhold our love from others, they experience this as deprivation, which it is. However, others also feel grief at the loss of the loved one. This feeling of loss, if not dealt with appropriately, often leads to denial and readily transforms into hatred and hurt.

The degree of hurt experienced, depends on several factors. Firstly, we can only be hurt if we allow others to hurt us. Secondly, during those times in our lives when we were not strong enough to prevent others from hurting us, we were vulnerable to hurt. If we were subjected to hurtful experiences in our formative years, we are likely to recreate this very basic dynamic with those who come close to us.

Thirdly, at the feeling level of interaction with those around us, love exists side by side with all other feelings, whatever they may be. It is a difficult concept to grasp, especially when you consider opposite feelings such as love and hate existing side by side.

Whatever the reality may be, if you have not been able to appreciate the richness of giving to others, then you may be likely to fall victim to one of the most important reasons as to why you hurt the ones you love the most. Namely, that you may resent having to give to the ones that you love. Giving, in this context can be an enriching experience. Especially, giving to those who you love the most.

19

the journey's end

The odds are that when you started this book, you were looking for some answers to questions that you have been unable to find elsewhere. I have found that if you have read a book with specific questions in mind, you are more likely to learn from that book.

You have come a long way since you started your journey. The fact is, you still have a long road ahead of you. The road we have journeyed together so far, will undoubtedly, lead you to many other roads. What you have to do is decide where you want to go from here.

As difficult as it may seem, someone else can't tell you which road to follow. This does not mean that you are alone. All this means is that you are responsible for whatever happens in your life. You have the freedom to exercise this responsibility as you wish.

The indicators of personal and social decay are increasing as time goes by. Every year there are more suicides, more abortions, more admissions to psychiatric facilities, more divorces, more bankruptcies, more homicides, more unemployment and less happiness.

So, what do we do? We need to open our eyes to see reality for what it is and open our minds to seek better ways of existing. Here are some suggestions. Truly happy people are honest, fair, decent, compassionate, loving and humane. They seek warm and loving relationships with others.

Self-destructive behaviour is not consistent with their actions and they avoid self-destructive people. They understand that the most important ingredient for their personal happiness is love. Love for their parents, children, partner, friends, humanity...

Truly happy people aim to achieve a balance in their lives. A balance that stems from a sense of moderation rather than dwelling on the extremities of life. Truly happy people volunteer unconditional love to those who love them. Their goal in life is to give of themselves to others in order to make this a better world for all of us.

Without the knowledge and insight offered to you, you were like the little stream; unable to continue your journey and fulfil your purpose in life. If you have read this book and feel ready to take responsibility for your life, that is great.

For some, it may be necessary to re-read this book several times. For others, it may be worthwhile to seek professional guidance to further explore the thoughts, ideas and feelings brought to the surface.

Your happiness is not going to drop down with the next rain. The world is full of people who are waiting. What are you waiting for? The choice is yours.

This is not the end. The end is when you take your last breath and you can't take anymore. So, between now and then, you have the option of making positive changes in your life. Here are some suggestions. You can start by responding to people rather than emotionally reacting to them. You can redefine your own foundations, values, beliefs and self and the foundations of your interpersonal relationships to include basic characteristics of honesty, respect, integrity, consistency, compassion, reciprocation and love.

You can acknowledge and become aware of the boundaries between what is inside your skin and your impact on the world around you and what is outside your skin and how the world impacts on you. You can slowly start rebuilding bridges with salvageable friendships and move on with others. You can start to bring closure to draining and one sided relationships and make a concerted effort to appreciate that the meaningful ones will make all the difference in your life.

Yes, YOUR life!

If I am not for myself, who will be for me?
I am for myself only, What am I?
If not now – when?

Talmudic Saying
Mishnah, Abot

Fearnot

Fearnot the high tides of life
That bury you deeper and deeper into the soil
from which you came,

Fearnot the treacherous and colourful rivers
That carry you further and further away
From your soul,

Fearnot death that beckons your last breath and
Holds your hand to the edge only
To watch you fall over,

Love not death but life.
Life is living.
Death is the rest.

Dr David Kaye

references

Aesop 1954, *Fables of Aesop*, Penguin Books, Harmonsworth, England

Bach, G. R., & Wyden, P. 1969, *The intimate enemy*, Morrow, New York

Bain, J. A. 1928, *Thought control in everyday life*, Funk & Wagnalls, New York

Balint, M. 'New beginning and the paranoid and depressive syndromes', in the *International Journal of Psycho-analysis*, 1952, 33, 214

Bellak, L. 1981, *Crises and special problems in psycho-analysis and psychotherapy*, Brunner/Mazel, New York

Beck, A. T. 1967, *Depression: Clinical, experimental and theoretical aspects*, Harper & Row, New York

Bergin, A.E., *'The effects of psychotherapy; negative results revisited'*, in the Journal of Counselling Psychology, 1963, 10, 244-250

Bernard, M.E. 1986, *Staying rational in an irrational world*, Macmillan Australia, Melbourne

Bowlby, J., 'The making and breaking of affectional bonds', in the *British Journal of Psychiatry*, 1977, 130, 201 & 431

Freud, S. 1920, *Beyond the pleasure principle*, Standard edition, Vol. XVIII, 7--64. Hogarth Press, London

Lazarus, A.A., 'New methods in psychotherapy: A case study', in the South *African Medical Journal*, 1958, 32, 660-664

Lazarus, A.A., 'Relationship therapy: often necessary but usually insufficient', in the *Counselling Psychologist*, 1969, 1, 25-27

Lazarus, A.A. 1971, *Behaviour therapy and beyond*, McGraw-Hill Book Company, New York

Malan, D. H. 1976, *The frontier of brief psychotherapy*, Plenum Press, New York

Malan, D. H. 1976, *Toward the validation of dynamic psychotherapy*, Plenum Press. New York

Malan, D. H. 1979, *Individual psychotherapy and the science of psychodynamics*, Butterworths, London

Marks, I. M. 1969, *Fears and phobias*, Academic Press, London

Orlinsky, D. E. & Howard, K. I., 'The good therapy

hour' in the *Archives of General Psychiatry*, 1967, 16, 621-632.

Phillipson, H. 1955, *The object relations technique*, Glencoe, III. The Free Press, Tavistock, London

Wolpe, J. 1958, *Psychotherapy by reciprocal inhibition*. Stanford, California

Wolpe, J. 1969, *The practice of behaviour therapy*, Pergamon, New York